MW01043241

Askia H. Bashir

HOW TO MANAGE YOUR PARENTS
(Without Manipulation)

Copyright 1995 by Askia H. Bashir
Published by KYD Publishers
Bilalian Production Incorporation
Atlanta, Georgia 30310

Library of Congress
Catalog number 95-82178
ISBN 0-9650628-0-5

Printed in the United States of America

For information on this book, write or call us at
Bilalian Productions Incorporation, KYD Publishers,
401 Hillside Drive S. W., Atlanta, Georgia 30310,

(404-752-8877),
between 9:00 A.M. and 6:00 P.M. EST

TABLE OF CONTENTS

Dedication & Acknowledgments 3

Introduction 5

PART 1 - The Concept of Upward Management 8

PART 2 - Parent and Child 16

PART 3 - Begin by Forgiving..26

PART 4 - Accepting Total Responsibility.............................30

PART 5 - Communication 33

PART 6 - Managing 46

PART 7 - Understanding Your Parents.................................63

PART 8 - Strategies for Managing.......................................73

PART 9 - Personal Development 80

PART 10 - Goal Setting...87

PART 11 - Becoming a Favorite Child.................................98

PART- 12 - Maintaining a Good Relationship.......................116
    The Seven Requirements for Success...................121

Summary..125

Epilogue..127

General Bibliography...129

Survey Form...133

With the name of God the beneficent, the merciful

DEDICATION
AND
ACKNOWLEDGMENTS

This book is dedicated to:
My Grandmother and Grandfather
Louise and Reno Martin

My Mother and Father
Mary and Hyron Pinson-Bashir

My Mother-in-Law and Father-in-Law
Guyulla and G. B. George

Atlena and Drellie Mathis, my aunt and uncle
and
My Wife Deborah

Mr. and Mrs. Edward & Mildred Johnson,
Educators Atlanta Public Schools
(Mays High School & Morris Brandon Elementary -
Atlanta, Georgia)

Linda (Betty) Allen -Stephens,
my cousin who taught me how to read.

Joyce Davis, City of Atlanta, Bureau of Training
(Who passed away on November 14, 1995)

And all of my supporters and friends
who encouraged me to complete this book.

Chief Editor, K.Anoa Monsho
Assisting Editors, Sonya Wyatt
Kimberlyn Griffin
Graphic Artist, Omar Rasheed

HOW TO MANAGE YOUR PARENTS
By: Askia H. Bashir
Introduction

Imagine a beautiful, healthy and harmonious relationship between you and your parents. Imagine getting your parents' approval and support to do the things you want to do! Imagine a peaceful, happy and loving feeling when you are with your parents. This is the relationship you can have when you know how to manage your parents.

For over 12 years I have been concerned with the unique elements that make family relationships successful, enjoyable and rewarding. I have studied relationships between parents and children. I have read many books on child rearing and the family. I have studied management, listened to taped seminars on the psychology of relationships, and I have conducted research with several different families on the subject of their relationships.

In addition to years of exhaustive study and research, my wife, Deborah, and I have reared eight children of our own over 25 years of marriage. This personal experience is one of the main reasons why I have spent countless hours studying techniques on "upward management." Now, I can share this knowledge with you.

Over the years, I have interviewed several mothers and fathers about their relationships with their children. In some cases, it was sad to see parents unable to get along with, and in some cases, even afraid of their children. It is even sadder to see children afraid of their parents, not knowing how to improve their relationships. Some families had reached a point where they gave up trying to understand one another. Many expressed frustration and anger. On the other hand, most parents also expressed the desire for their children to be happy and successful in life and as well as obedient. They felt that it was not too much to ask that their children respect them and strive to succeed. I agree.

But, have we given children real instructions on how to get along with their parents? Have we given them the tools to work with so they can live up to parental expectations? According to biblical scripture, parents should: " *Train a child in the way that he should go and when he is old, he will not depart from it.* " It is the parents'

5

obligation to train their children.

The information contained in this book is helpful to every child. And please do not be offended when I use the word child. The term is not meant to belittle you or to make you feel immature or incompetent or even a certain age. Because, whether you are sixteen or sixty, as long as you live, you are your parents' child.

This book is intended to help train you in the skills you will need to manage your relationship with your parents. In this book, I will show you an innovative concept and some basic techniques that, if you apply them, will improve your life. You will be more effective, successful and happy as you learn to manage the most important relationship in your life. I will show you, through a step-by-step process of instructions, how to take control of your life and improve your relationship with your mother and father. Using this new concept of managing, you will be able to get along with your parents, get what you want from them, and get ahead in life. Your personal, social and family relations will be enhanced. Never again will you feel powerless or hopeless when it comes to your relationship with your parents. With my "win-win philosophy," you will be able to get your parents to agree to everything you need and may want to do. You will be completely satisfied and so will they.

This book is not about managing your parents through intimidation. It is not about taking advantage of anyone. It is not about manipulating situations or controlling your parents in any way. *When you manage your parents, your objective is to experience a win-win harmonious outcome.* Both you and your parents will benefit from these positive experiences. But in order for these techniques to be successful, there are two things you must understand. The first is that you must accept total responsibility for the relationship. Second, realize that you are in control of your own destiny.

In the past, there hasn't been enough information available about upward management in successful relationships. Some people just seemed lucky that their relationships worked out. Well, luck has very little to do with it. Whether they were aware of it or not, people who enjoy good relationships with their parents are using techniques you'll find in this book. After you read it, there'll be no excuse for not having an excellent relationship with your mom and dad.

As you mature, you will understand that you cannot have a successful and happy life without positive relationships. This book will help you transform the most important relationship of your life.

Resolve to spend time learning to manage your parents. You will reap tremendous benefits from the effort you invest.

I have asked God Almighty to guide my thoughts during the writing of this book, and I have asked Him to give you the "good" contained in each part. Congratulations! Just taking the time to read this book is the first step to your sucess. Peace be with you and much happiness for the rest of your life.

PART 1

THE CONCEPT OF UPWARD MANAGEMENT

In the corporate world, major emphasis is placed on management. When an effective management system is operating within a business, the business's goals and objectives are met and business thrives.

Today many corporations are exploring the concept of upward management. It is taught in seminars, workshops and universities across the country. In the corporate environment, upward management is a process that encourages the subordinate to manage the boss. Instead of the boss telling the subordinate what to do, the subordinate is allowed to suggest to his or her boss what needs to be done. After reading about this concept and understanding its dynamics, I believe this process will work with children and their parents. Instead of parents telling their children what to do, children are empowered to suggest the things they need and want to do. That's what upward management is all about. The amazing thing about this process is that both managers and parents like to be managed when suggestions are made to them in a positive and progressive way.

INNOVATIVE

Ralph Waldo Emerson said, "Society is taken by surprise at any new example of common sense." If I simply told you that you needed a good relationship with your parents, you would probably agree but never give any serious thought as to how to develop such a relationship. Judging from the quality of relationships in many families, children give little thought to developing a good relationship with their parents. Yet, my years of research and work on the subject of parent management have convinced me that those who enjoy pleasant relationships with their parents do so because of their cooperation and willingness to learn. They want to improve in basic areas that others may take for granted. How parents feel about their children is a key factor in a winning relationship.

Children who work to improve the way their parents feel about them simply have better relationships and get more of what they want from those relationships. Yet most children have never thought about how they would benefit from better relationships with their parents.

CONCERNS AND THE NEED FOR INFORMATION

I heard many comments from parents and children regarding how they felt about each other. Things like:

" My child is sending us through a lot of changes right now..."

"My son is acting pretty crazy in school."

"My child doesn't care for me as much as I care for him."

"My daughter is beginning to act wild."

"Her hormones are acting up..."

"Lord, please help us with our children."

"He's insensitive..."

"She's unappreciative and uncaring."

"He has left home and is staying with someone else."

Many young people made the following comments about their parents:

"My mother won't let me do anything anymore."

"I just fell out with my mother and father about..."

"I have to get their permission for everything. I should be

able to do what I want to do. I can think."

"They are unreasonable..."

"Overbearing! Intimidating! Patronizing! Inflexible!"

"I can't wait to get out on my own!"

"They won't let me live my own life, won't listen, overprotective..

No one wants to be described in any of these ways and if these perceptions exist in your family, you can do something about it.

After listening to parents and children talk about each other, I concluded that unless children are given the information they need to manage their parents, these relationships will continue to deteriorate.

The practical concept of managing your parents entails active compassion, patience, kindness, appreciation and respect for them. Your parents have the right to expect you to be obedient in return for what they have done for you. *However, if parents encourage injustice or wrongdoing or ask you to do something improper or illegal, disobedience becomes not only justifiable but a duty. Do not submit to abuse or wrongdoing of any sort. You have a God-given right to resist wrong treatment or any injustice.*

You can learn to manage your parents by examining your current relationship with them and applying the techniques in the following chapters. In my research I learned that, in most cases, if you make a good impression on your parents, you can get what you want. If you make a poor impression, you will have problems. When you choose not to follow your parents' advice, you may end up in trouble. It's that simple. The more you become aware of how important parents are to your success in life, the more you'll want to know about how to manage them. Once you recognize the need to skillfully manage your parents, it becomes crucial for you to acquire the knowledge to meet the challenges.

The Bible says, *"Wisdom is the principal thing; therefore get wisdom: and with all thy getting get understanding."*

Managing your parents is an art that must be customized for you,

10

your parents and your circumstances. The strategy is to create an environment that helps make mom and dad better parents, and that means giving you the support and independence you need to grow.

PRINCIPLES OF MANAGING YOUR PARENTS

There are five major principles involved in managing your parents. They are:

- *Believe the Creator meant for you to have a good relationship with your parents.*

- *Obey your parents and show gratitude.*

- *Be proactive.*

- *Be responsible for the relationship with your parents.*

- *Treat your parents in a positive, sincere and genuine way.*

WHAT'S IN IT FOR YOU AND THEM

You might think that managing your parents will take a lot of extra time and effort and you are not sure the relationship is worth it. Well, the extra time and effort you put into managing your parents will have a tremendous payoff. Here's why:

- *It shows your parents that you really care about them. Parents will listen to what you say, but they believe what they see. If you want to find out what they believe, watch what they do. And when they want to find out what you believe, they watch what you do. The more you can show your parents that you are mature and responsible, the more readily they will perceive you that way.*

- *You will acquire a sense of pride and confidence. When you put forth effort to learn and respond to your parents' needs, you have the assurance of knowing that you can help them and give them a reason to trust you.*

11

- *Quality relationships make you feel great! Put yourself in your parents' shoes. Would you like for your children to treat you with disrespect and disobedience? Or would you like your children to be appreciative, grateful and obedient? Evidence shows that the relationship between parent and child is good when the child makes the effort to please the parent.*

- *It overcomes defensive behavior and gains support for you. If your parents have concerns which cause them to be upset with you, you can easily say, "Yes, ma'am (or sir), I am listening, I'd like to correct this situation."*

- *You'll stop thinking that your parents like someone else better than you. If you've ever had a bad relationship with your parents, you may have heard them make comments about some other person's success. When you know more about your parents and how to manage them, your parents begin to see you as a role model.*

GOD AND PARENTS, TWO OF OUR GREATEST ASSETS

Stop for a moment and consider just how valuable your parents are. With God's help, they make it possible for you to grow up, become educated, earn a living, and start your own families. Your obedience, respect and successful accomplishments will give them reasons to continue supporting you. All the money in the world is no substitute for happiness, love and a loving family. Don't ever make the mistake of thinking that money, cars, homes and jobs are your greatest assets. Every child's greatest assets are God and his parents. Without these, there is no life.

Throughout this book, you will be reminded how important acquiring knowledge is. And that *Knowledge is power if you remember to use it.*

OUR DUTY AND RESPONSIBILITY

What are the most significant reasons that you can think of for improving your relationship with your parents? Several come to my mind.

12

Some are from the Bible, such as:

- *"Honor thy father and thy mother: that thy days may be long upon the land which the Lord thy God giveth thee."*   *Exodus 20:12*

- *"Children, obey your parents in the Lord; for this is right." Ephesians 6:1*

And some are from the Qur'an:

- *"And thy Lord has decreed that you worship none but him, and that ye be kind to parents. Whether one or both of them attain old age in thy life, say not to them a word of contempt, nor repel them, but address them in terms of honor." 17:23*

- *"And out of kindness lower to them the wing of humility, and say my Lord, bestow on them thy mercy even as they cherished me in childhood." 17:24*

- *"We have enjoined on man kindness to his parents. In pain did his mother bear him, and in pain did she give him birth. The carrying of the child to his weaning is a period of thirty months. At length, when he reaches the age of full strength and attains forty years, he says, O my Lord ! Grant me that I may be grateful for thy favor which thy has bestowed upon me and both my parents..." 31:14*

- *"And reverence the wombs that bore you for God watches over you." 4:1*

These statements indicate that we have received guidance from our Creator to honor, obey, show appreciation and respect our parents. What will be the direct benefit to you for obeying your parents? Long days, a long life in this world.

Everyone, no matter what, wants to live as long as he or she can to be successful. Your days can be extended and God's mercy shown to you, if you are obedient to your parents. Why should you obey your parents? Because God commands you to obey them. If you can

13

think of a thousand reasons why you should obey your parents, remember that God's command to you is sufficient enough. No matter how young or old you are, be aware of your responsibility. It is God who designed for you to have a good relationship with your parents. It is His command.

A WIN-WIN OUTCOME !

God has commanded you to respect and honor your parents but have you thought about how to go about it? You have the opportunity to determine how your parents respond to you. But remember, all efforts to manage your parents must be sincere and genuine. *And please, let me emphasize being sincere and genuine. If you are not sincere and genuine, managing your parents will not work!*

When I mention managing your parents, I am not suggesting that you try in any way to maneuver or manipulate them. Rather, the term is used to mean *the process of consciously working with your parents to obtain the best possible results for all parties through obedience, cooperation and good deeds.* Some of your objectives include being truthful, enthusiastic, sincere and genuine. In a very real way, you are managing one of the most important relationships you will ever have.

TRADITION

Managing your parents may sound unusual or even suspicious because of the traditional way children are reared. Parents manage their children with "downward" instructions. It is a traditional and accepted practice that parents tell their children what to do. Right now, it may not be obvious why you need to manage the relationship "upward" so that you suggest to your parents what is to be done. Understanding upward management will make things clear and easy for you.

Have you ever wondered why some of your friends have great relationships with their parents and how others can't seem to find the formula to get along with theirs? Just what happens in successful relationships that is not happening in unsuccessful ones? If you asked families why they are or aren't successful, each would give a different answer. However, everyone wants their family relationships to be happy. How can you improve your relationship with your parents? Simple. Make a decision to manage that relationship by changing your attitude for the better.

MAKE A DECISION TO CHANGE

From this point on, you must make a decision to change for the better. Change has to take place in you before you will see a change in others. Make a commitment to be truthful, honest and sincere with your parents no matter what! Think of yourself as having your slate wiped absolutely clean and starting brand new. Most people get only one opportunity to make a first impression. Give yourself another chance to make a first impression on your parents by starting the process of managing them now!

SPEAK THE TRUTH
REGARDLESS OF THE CIRCUMSTANCES

Always speak the truth. When you speak the truth, you are perceived as honest and looked upon as a person of integrity. If you commit yourself to this principle of being truthful and honest, you can gain the respect, cooperation and trust of most people.

PART 2

PARENT AND CHILD

In order to understand how to manage your parents, you must first define parent and child. What is a parent? What is a child?

PARENT - is a father or mother. There are two types of parents, biological and adoptive parents. A child's biological parents are the man and woman who physically produced that child. Adoptive parents are the persons who assume the responsibility and care for a particular child that is not their biological offspring. All parents should contribute to the mental and physical care of their children, including provisions for food, clothing, shelter, love, discipline and protection.

In the beginning of your life, your parents were not dependent on you. You were dependent on them. Parents should not be an interruption in your life. They should help you find your purpose in your life. *You are doing yourself a favor by obeying them.* Parents are not people you argue or match wits with, but those whom you can talk to. Parents bring requests in form of compliance and it is your job to handle those requests in a positive way. Society often takes the place of parents if you are not careful. Television programs, peer pressure, or even correctional institutions can rear you if you do not have the guidance of real parents.

CHILD - is a person of either sex; offspring or descendent. As long as you live, you are your parents' child. *But, for the sake of managing your parents, a child is anyone who is age 13 or older.* The 13 and over age group was selected because persons who are 12 years and younger may not be able to apply the techniques recommended in this book. However, young people are encouraged to read this book for ideas they can apply.

Usually when a child reaches the age of 13, their desire to become independent increases. Some children mature faster than others, and in most cases, the female matures faster than the male.

Understanding the changes in your life during this time allows you to begin understanding the importance of giving more to your parents, rather than expecting to receive more from them. Your parents bring you into this world. You are nurtured and raised by them until early adulthood. You spend countless hours with them directly and indirectly. You are with them directly in the home, and indirectly at social, religious, school and business activities. You have a lot at stake in the relationship. Whether your relationship is good or bad, it impacts directly on your personal, and often, your professional life. Your parents control much of what you do until you leave their home. Even after you leave home, you may still need their financial support, advice, and wisdom. A good parental relationship goes a long way toward increasing your happiness and success in life.

IS YOUR RELATIONSHIP IN DANGER?

Changing social and economic times have distracted many parents and children from being close to one another. Are you in danger of destroying the relationship with your parents? If you want to find out, stop for a moment and ask yourself these questions:

- *Are you hanging out with people who are always in trouble?*

- *Are you acting secretly by hiding your friends and activities from your parents?*

- *Are you drinking alcohol, using, or possessing drugs?*

- *Do you have behavior problems in school or in your community?*

- *Do you experience extreme mood swings?*

- *Are you committing petty theft and becoming anti-sociable?*

- *Are you disregarding your parents' curfew hours and other established home rules?*

If you answered "yes" to any of these questions, you may be destroying your relationship with your mom and dad.

Recent studies done in reference to "at-risk youth" indicate that, *as parents, we must recognize the importance of our roles in these challenging times. Too many children today are not experiencing the "golden period" of freedom before the tensions of the adult world seize them. Many experts say childhood is dead. It is killed by any number of assailants within a society that does not protect and cherish its youngest members; by a culture that no longer celebrates the joyous rituals of childhood. Although childhood may appear to have died, the children survived!*

One study also revealed that parents spend roughly 17 hours of interaction per week with their children, 15 minutes of quality time with their spouses, and 30 seconds of quality time with their children. Children watch an average of seven hours of television every day. A significant number of today's youth are technologically overstimulated, spiritually bankrupt and emotionally isolated from any support system that could help them understand today's complex problems. Today's youth show less emotion, devalue life, and are lonely, fearful and anxious. They seek life-threatening adventures and events to excite and stir their emotions. Lesser challenges will not do.

According to another study, 92 percent of all comprehensive learning takes place outside the classroom. *There are studies indicating that up to about ten hours of TV viewing a week correlates with improved school achievement, while more viewing time correlates with lower achievement. During children's hours, 90 percent of the programs were violent. Over 25 violent acts an hour are committed during the weekend daytime children's programming. The trend is toward increased cartoon violence.*

Some trends are positive and some are not. Trends come from all parts of the country, especially the states of ***California, Florida, Texas, Washington, Colorado and Connecticut.*** Pay attention to trends, fads and the influences coming from these areas. If you are sharp, you can use this knowledge to successfully avoid trouble.

OTHER INFLUENCES

Music from so-called entertainers, violent and sexually explicit movies, videos, and virtual reality games, are definite contributing factors to failing relationships. Messages of anti-social behavior are having a negative impact on today's youth. Parents and children struggle with many challenges brought on by outside influences. Be aware of these influences so you will be better able to understand and cooperate with your parents when they suggest that you shouldn't listen to or watch certain types of music or television. Remember, your parents have been in many of the same places, predicaments and circumstances that you are trying to deal with. Recognize that you need to listen to them when they give you advice. Adopt an attitude of cooperation instead of resistance.

IDENTIFIED AREAS OF IMPROVEMENT

Most problems between the parents and children are caused by incompatibility due to lack of interpersonal and management skills. One of your goals must be to improve your interpersonal skills and abilities. This will improve the compatibility and allegiance between you and your parents.

SHOW APPRECIATION

If you are going to be successful in improving the quality of your life, you must show appreciation for your parents' contributions to you. Without your parents you would not exist. You would not be reading this book. You could not get angry or be happy with them, or make decisions on a day-to-day basis as you do. It is critical that you understand the "gift of life" from your parents. The Creator gave parents the ability to bring you into this world! They have given you the opportunity to live, to develop yourself, and to exercise your full potential as a human being.

Your parents make daily sacrifices in order to rear you. The commitment they make to see you be successful as an adult is absolutely incredible! Think about it. For them, there is no more single life. No more carefree, happy go lucky days where all they have to think about is themselves and what they want to do with their lives. You have become their major concern and interest from the moment you were born.

Whether employed or unemployed, educated or illiterate, healthy or sick, young or old, happy or sad, your parents find some way to provide for you the best they know how. Not only do they provide the basics, they also provide some luxuries. Know for certain that your parents need to be appreciated and respected for all the things they willingly do for you.

THEY DO IT ALL FOR YOU

One of the most gratifying experiences for a parent is to see his or her child be successful, promising, and appreciative, even in the slightest way. Remember that all of their aspirations and dreams are represented through you. It makes them happy to see you succeed and it disappoints them when you are not realizing your highest potential.

In fact, when my children do something that is positive and progressive, my wife and I are very pleased, proud and happy. You do not have to worry about doing the big things in life to make your parents proud. Many times it is just the little things that count and can make a big difference.

When I say that your parents want you to be successful, I mean an ongoing success. That does not mean achieving a goal and stopping. It is a continuous process. Success does not mean having what someone else has or achieves. Success is the constant achievement of worthwhile goals. Take the attitude that "if it's to be, it's up to me" and that success is an individual experience. So, do not measure yourself by the accomplishments of others. Success means to give it your best effort, learn, grow and be willing to continue the pursuit of positive perfection, even though you make mistakes. Success is a life-long process. Once you succeed at an activity or goal, it is important that you continue to grow and improve your condition and yourself by setting new expectations.

THEY LOVE AND CARE FOR YOU

Parents need to see you being successful. It is the positive feedback of seeing your successes that encourages parents to work harder for you!

They will give you support, encouragement, love and affection when they see you being successful, happy, respectful and apprecia-

20

tive. Forgiveness and generosity are the direct results of parents seeing your success. When you are successful, it makes them feel terrific!

FOUR STRATEGY STATEMENTS

On the next few pages, you are going to become familiar with the valuable principles and requirements that work in parent management. You may already be using some of these principles, and if you are, great! You already know some things that work.

Much of the value in this book is contained in the four strategy statements of managing your parents. They are:

- *Ask not what your parents can do for you, ask what you   can do for your parents.*

- *It is your responsibility to manage your parents in order to achieve an effective relationship.*

- *You determine, and are responsible for your own destiny.*

- *You have an obligation to establish and maintain an excellent relationship with your parents.*

TAKING THE LEAD

If you are waiting for your mother and father to lead the way and make all the decisions, you are headed in the wrong direction. If you are waiting for your parents to understand you before you understand them, things are not going to work out as they should.

You take the lead. Ask yourself, "What can I do? What would make mom and dad happy, right now?" The answer will probably be to adjust your attitude. When you do that, your parents will not be able to resist the *"new and improved"* you. Find ways to make yourself better. Find solutions instead of dwelling on problems. Know that you have control over your own destiny, because you are now the manager. Contribute to the relationship by doing as much as you can for your parents.

PROACTIVE

The best attitude is a proactive attitude. Proactive is the opposite of reactive. A proactive person is someone with vision and anticipation of circumstances and consequences. This person develops ideas, plans, and actions to make sure that circumstances come out in their favor in a timely manner. For instance, if you wanted to borrow something from your parents, and presuming that you have a good relationship with them already, make sure that:

- *What you want to borrow is available.*

- *The time you want to borrow it doesn't conflict with them or their time.*

- *You tell them the time you will return it and do so, on time.*

- *You arrange a service for what you borrow (if necessary).*

- *A verbal request is made ahead of time and your intentions explained.*

- *You ask for their decision as soon as they feel comfortable with the arrangements.*

- *You stay on good terms with them during the waiting period and afterwards.* ***Especially if they say "no."***

TAKE THE INITIATIVE

Sit down with your parents, and give them a number of areas in which you intend to improve. At once, you will notice their surprise at your proactive attitude. Expect a look of surprise from them as well as curiosity, a smile, support, encouragement, agreement, and questions. Once they have finished reacting to this wonderful news, shake their hands as though you have just executed the greatest contract in your life. Make this beginning a personal one by giving them a warm hug. Again, be ready for their positive reaction, because of your positive proactive attitude.

WORK SMART AND HARD

"Surely after difficulty comes ease. Surely after difficulty comes ease. But when thy immediate task has been removed, still strive hard." This saying from the Qur'an reminds us that after difficulty, hard work and sacrifice, come good times to be experienced. At the same time, the saying also reminds people to maintain what they have accomplished by guarding their profits, the product, or the good times, after all the hard work and dedication.

When things are not the way they should be, there's an opportunity to be proactive. When things are the way they should be, ask yourself, "Is there anything else I can do to improve my conditions? What is it I can do to make sure everything is going the right way?" This is the proactive attitude you want to develop and refine.

THE INVESTMENT

These are just some basic steps that can be taken to improve your success of getting what you want. Imagine the relationship with your parents as that of a bank. Imagine using "yes dollars" instead of real dollars to set up an account in your "relationship bank". Now, imagine your parents as the merchants you want to buy from. The "yes dollars" can be used for making "yes purchases" from your parents' store. Your parents' store sells "yes responses". The "yes responses" come in the form of approval, permission, and cooperation. In order to earn "yes dollars", you must do something they want *without being told.*

Think of as many ways as you can to earn "yes dollars" to deposit into the bank. And write them down so they can be used again and again. Assume that the only way you can earn "yes dollars" is to do something positive and proactive that your parents want done. Once you accumulate your "yes dollars", you can spend them as you would spend real dollars. The difference is you will spend your "yes dollars" on getting your parents' permission, approval or cooperation for the things you want. You need to know approximately what that permission or approval will cost.

Remember, mom and dad keep a mental record of your actions and attitudes. It may take more "yes dollars" to earn a favorable response in one area than in another. Be an accountant and manager of your resources. This imaginary illustration is useful if you consider your relationship with your parents as an investment. One objective in managing your parents is to get them to say "yes", and keep them saying "yes" to your needs with a win-win outcome. Being proactive allows you to make the deposits in advance for future uses.

LIKE THEM!

Do you like your parents? If so, show interest in their life and accomplishments and let them know you are proud that they are your parents. If you don't genuinely like your parents, they will not feel the need to cooperate with you. What can help you learn to like your parents more? Try to get to know them. The more you know about your parents, the more you can find reason to admire them. Parents are not perfect, and you aren't either. Look at the good things they do and have done for you. This will always exceed, by far, their negative deeds. Show gratitude, respect, and recognize your parents for their admirable efforts. With very little effort, it is easy for you to find out what your parents want to be recognized for. Look at their professional or civic accomplishments, their weight control, good advice, a new dress or suit they may be wearing. Comment, and ask questions. "Mom, are you controlling weight? You look good and fit. Dad, is that a new tie you're wearing? It looks sharp with those shoes..." Be honest about your observations. Think before you speak.

Make your parents feel comfortable around you. You like to be around people who accept you and make you feel relaxed. Do you ever wonder why some families seem to get along and enjoy being around each other? Be sociable. How can you improve in this area? Psychologists give several reasons for behaviors that contribute to developing rapport. Take a look at this list for ways to improve.

- *Talk to your parents about what's going on in your life. Discuss movies, books and music with them. Ask them   about their lives and concerns.*

- *Give a genuine smile.*

- *Stand or sit in a relaxed and comfortable manner.*

- *Look people in the eye.* (If you feel uncomfortable looking people in the eye, look at their foreheads. They won't be able to tell the difference.)

- *Lean toward people and show interest in what they are saying or doing.*

- *Make genuine and timely touches. Hug, shake hands, or even kiss them when appropriate.*

- *Remember relatives' names as much as possible, and use their names when referring to them.*

- *Blend in with people. Don't be an oddball by isolating yourself.*

You can also enhance rapport by using clean and timely humor. People like to laugh. If they are laughing, this means they are listening to what you are saying. This is a very good time to impress them with your ideas. Every family member benefits when your relationship improves.

PART 3

BEGIN BY FORGIVING

You might be thinking, "This is all great, but how do I begin?" When you ask this question, you are definitely on your way. You have arrived at the most important step, the beginning. Begin with the concept of reprogramming your mind for positive and good changes. ___The decision to___ ___change is the beginning.___ Say to yourself, "I want the relationship with my parents to be better than it is." Say, "I will improve my relationship with my parents and I forgive them." You must have the desire, the will and a determined mind to succeed with mom and dad.

The mind is the mechanism that determines your behavior, feelings, and desires. It is said that "As a man thinkth, so is he." Your mind is where you will start to make changes. You come into the world as an empty vessel. You are taught how to do most everything. When you are taught, this means that you are trained or programmed by someone or something in a direct or indirect way. You receive formal training from your first teacher - your mother, and then from your father. You continue to receive formal training from teachers and instructors in your schools, colleges and universities. You receive informal training through your interactions with other human beings and the environment. In fact, some people think that radio, television and video games are contributing more to your mental programming than schools, colleges and universities.

ASKING FOR FORGIVENESS

Forgiveness is an important first step in managing your parents. Ask God, the Creator, to help and to forgive you. God is most forgiving and merciful. You are very limited in your capacity to forgive others because you are human and you have limitations. If someone does something to you, you have a tendency to want justice, revenge, or some kind of compensation. God is above all of your human experiences. God cannot be hurt, disappointed, or surprised. God is all-knowing and totally independent of any need or any thing.

26

God has the capability to forgive you for your errors and wrongdoing in life. Ask God to forgive you for every evil, bad, and stupid thing you have ever done in your life.

And, as the Bible says, "Forgive our trespassers as we forgive those who trespass against us." Ask the Creator for clemency and to make you successful with your parents.

FORGIVING YOUR PARENTS

The next step is to forgive your parents. Forgiveness is the glue that repairs relationships. Forgiveness is better than punishment, because forgiveness heals the hurt. Forgive your parents for every bad, evil, stupid mistake or thing they have ever done to you or others. It is said *"To err is human, to forgive is divine."* Forgiving your parents allows the healing and the recovery process to begin if you have been hurt or disappointed by your parents. I want you to take one minute and repeat to yourself over and over again, "I forgive my parents." You may have some doubt about whether or not this process will actually work, especially if you do not have a good relationship with your parents. Nevertheless, repeat this exercise at least five times a day whenever you can for thirty days. You will begin to feel better almost instantly. Remember, *you are responsible for your relationship* with your parents. Focus on forgiving, being positive, proactive and successful. *Forgiveness is a balm that heals relationships.* Let go of the past and allow healing to take place within your family.

FORGIVING OTHERS

You will also need to forgive others. This can be very challenging. I know there are some people who may have done some terrible things to you. Remember, forgiveness is better than punishment if forgiveness correct the situation. Forgiveness releases you from your pain and anger . When you forgive, you are healing yourself. When you forgive others, it does not mean that you have to be their friend, or ever have anything to do with them. You do not have to be around them and you don't have to tell them that you forgive them. It doesn't matter if they are aware or not of your clemency. It only means that you are free of those negative thoughts which are counterproductive to *your* mental health. Forgive them and let go of the past so that you can move forward with your life. If you have done something in your life to offend and hurt others, it may be best that you apologize to them at a time or place when it is appropriate.

This provides an opportunity for others to forgive you. To be forgiven by others is also important. So, apologize to others for your wrong doing or mistakes.

FORGIVING YOURSELF

Finally, forgive yourself. Yes, forgive yourself for every evil, bad and stupid mistake or thing you have ever done in your entire life. You finish this important process by forgiving yourself, which then allows you to have a new beginning.

THE FORGIVING PROCESS AND RESULTS

When you ask for forgiveness, forgive your parents, forgive others and yourself, you are letting go of the ugly, unpleasant and unnecessary burdens of the memories or bad experiences that stop you from being happy. It takes a tremendous amount of effort to be unhappy, or angry with someone. In fact, it is unnatural to be angry or unhappy. Being happy is easy and effortless. If you are unhappy or angry with someone or about something, notice what you are thinking. Your mind has to think about the negatives in order for you to feel negative or unhappy about a particular person or circumstance.

Holding on to bad experiences and memories is like driving your car with the brakes on. You can and will make some progress, but your brakes, engine, transmission and other systems in your car will eventually be destroyed sooner than later. If you hold onto the ugly past or negative thoughts, it will eventually wear down your body and mind.

Holding on to negative experiences is also like wearing ankle weights. Ankle weights place stress on the legs and weigh them down. Even though you can step, jump or even run, your movement is slower. Your reaction time is slower. You use more energy and strength to perform routine leg functions. When you remove the ankle weights, it feels as if you can walk freer, jump higher, and run faster. When you remove negative experiences from your life, it is as if you have taken off unnecessary weight.

By removing the unnecessary weight, you remove a burden that pulls you down and restricts you from exercising your full potential. Negative thoughts and grudges will disappear if you just forgive others and let go of negative experiences. If you continue to hold on to negative thoughts, which actually produce poisons in the body, the result may be stress, high blood pressure, ulcers, depression and other dis-eases.

FORGIVING AND THE CHALLENGE

You are probably thinking that forgiveness is easier said than done. How do you get rid of negative thoughts, experiences and grudges? Imagine negativity as a tree with roots, trunk, branches and leaves. In order to kill any part of that tree, you just simply cut off the supply of food to that tree. Forgiving and accepting total responsibility for your own condition and actions cut out the roots of the tree of negativity. This will be challenging. You may have to grit your teeth and say with feeling to yourself, "I am responsible. I am responsible. I am responsible," over and over again until you stop blaming others for your circumstances.

Accept total responsibility for your destiny and let go of the ugly past right now! Practice the mental exercise of repeating over and over again, "I forgive my parents, others and myself." This mental exercise will reinforce the understanding that you are in control. Then, you can truly forgive and stop blaming others for your lack of peace and happiness. You can accept and become fully responsible for your success in life.

By beginning to use this mental exercise you will be well on your way to managing your family relationships. And finally, when you master exercising forgiveness, you will feel as did Dr. Martin Luther King, Jr.; "Free at last, free at last. Thank God the Almighty, we're free at last."

PART 4

ACCEPTING TOTAL RESPONSIBILITY

Michael Jackson, recorded a song that said, **"Don't blame it on the sunshine, don't blame it on the moonlight, don't blame it on the good times..."** Blaming people or circumstances for your condition only denies you the opportunity to become the best you can be. Think of situations where you may have refused to accept total responsibility. Usually, these situations caused your parents to be disappointed because of your irresponsibility.

You may feel your parents are always telling you what to do. Perhaps it's because you have not taken the initiative to direct yourself and the relationship. Accept total responsibility. Take the initiative to change the negatives into positives, and they will stop telling you what to do. Accept full responsibility for the relationship and you will see immediate progress.

WHO'S RESPONSIBLE?

After examining relationships between children and their parents, I have come to one clear understanding. Children are responsible for 51 percent or more of the quality of their family relationships. The parent/child relationship is complementary. Parents and children are mutually bound together with obligations and commitments. You will learn to accept more and more responsibility for managing your relationship as you refine and practice your skills.

THE NEED TO ACCEPT RESPONSIBILITY

When I question people about who is responsible for problems in the parent/child relationship, I get interesting answers. When I asked children, they invariably said the parents are to blame because they don't listen or take them seriously. When I asked parents, they said the child is not behaving and so it is the child's fault. Children are of the opinion that parents are in control of everything. On the other hand, parents expect their children to do what they tell them to do.

Thus, no one is taking responsibility and the relationship gets worse.

You might be thinking that things are really bad between you and your parents and you may not believe you can ever have a good relationship with them. You might think that if you did accept the challenge to create a better relationship, it wouldn't last very long. There are too many problems, too much bad blood, too many things that have been done to you, and too many things that you have done to them. And anyway, why should you be totally responsible for the relationship?

I interviewed a young man about his relationship with his parents. I asked him how well he got along with each parent. He indicated that his relationship with his father was okay. But, his mother was not as understanding as his father. I asked him to explain. He said, "When I come in late from a party or someplace, she gets mad and jumps all over me. When I don't do well in school, she gets upset. I can get into a little trouble, and she'll just go off!"

I asked him to stop and think for a moment, and give me some ways he could have improved the situations. At first, he continued to blame his mother for the negative condition of their relationship. I repeated the question. "What could you have done to make the situation better?" Slowly, he began to understand.

He realized that his behavior was the reason his mother was upset with him. "I should have been back at the time she expected me to be back. I could have called her to tell her I would be late or asked her if I could stay out longer" he admitted. "What about your grades in school," I asked, "Should your parents expect for you to do well in school?" "Yes" he said. "Do you have a problem in learning?" I asked. He quickly responded "No." Then tell me, I said, "What could you have done to make your situation better?" He answered, "I could have completed all of the work assignments that I was expected to do. I could have completed them, but for some reason, I didn't." "What about you getting in to trouble," I continued. "It was me who got in trouble each time. It was my mother who was concerned about me getting out of trouble, and caring for my future....I see what you are talking about," he admitted.

WHY DO YOUR PARENTS GET UPSET?

Why do your parents get upset with you? In most instances, it's because you disappoint them by not living up to their expectations. Or you hurt their feelings. How would you react if you were the parent? You would probably be disappointed too, if you didn't get what you expected.

In each of the young man's situations that he described his mother as not understanding or getting upset, he admitted his actions provoked her. Remember, people react to the way they are treated. Their reaction may or may not be what you expected. So be careful how you treat others.

PART 5

COMMUNICATION

SENDING YOUR MESSAGE

Communication is probably the most important skill you can ever learn in life. You must communicate to your parents, your intention to improve your relationship. Understanding communication is a vital key to managing your parents. Let's look at the definition of "communication" to find out how familiar you are with its meaning, usage, and importance.

Communication - to impart, share, make common; that which can be transmitted; said of thoughts; to make known; to give and receive information, signals, signs or messages; to be connected. A giving or receiving of information by signals, signs, music or messages by talking.

Considering these definitions, it's clear that there's more than one way to communicate. The object of communication is to deliver a message so that it can be understood. It serves as a means of sharing important information and in getting people to respond in certain ways.

Good communication skills can improve all your relationships. It is your responsibility to communicate in a way that helps your parents understand you and it is also your responsibility to make an effort to understand what your parents are trying to communicate to you.

THE MESSAGE, SENDER AND RECEIVER

In communication, there is a message or signal to be sent to someone. There must be someone to send or deliver the message. Once you have the message and a sender, you must have someone to receive the message. These are the three components of communication: *message, sender,* and *receiver.* If the party sending and the party receiving the message do not communicate very well, miscommunication occurs and the relationship will suffer. The ability to communicate is necessary in every field of endeavor, wherever people are trying to work together. Your progress depends on how well you

33

and your parents understand each other.

A misunderstanding in communication can lead to confusion dislike, enmity, hatred or, in some cases, even physical violence. Be aware of this. It is far wiser for you to think about your own skills when it comes to communication than to think of someone else's shortcomings.

There are three ways communication conveys ideas from one to another:

1. *Talking and listening.*
2. *Writing and reading.*
3. *Nonverbal communication;*
   body language.

In each one of the stated forms of communication, one person sends a message and another receives it. Regardless of the process used, in order to be effective, communication requires considerable skills. Each of these skills has to be learned, studied, and put into practice.

BECOMING SKILLED IN COMMUNICATION

There are five basic skills necessary for any person who needs to communicate to or direct the activities of others. That person must be able to:

1. *Speak clearly.*
2. *Listen.*
3. *Write clearly.*
4. *Read with understanding.*
5. *Understand basic body language.*

LISTENING

Of the skills involved in the communication process, most people seem to have the greatest trouble with listening. Many people assume that listening is the same as hearing, and that anyone who can hear can also listen. However, this is not the case. Listening not only requires that you hear, but also that you understand what you hear. To do this you must think about what the other person is saying as they are talking to you. Your parents may not be skillful in getting their message across. Pay close attention to what they are saying.

To be an effective listener requires that you become an active listener. Focus so that you can understand what your parents are saying. This means that you cannot be thinking of what you are going to say as soon as there's a pause. Think about what your parents are saying. This technique requires some practice if you have not tried it before, especially if you are anxious to "talk back" and get your own ideas across. Sometimes when you try to do all the talking, it causes you to miss what your parents are saying.

Devote more attention to listening. There are three key questions you should keep in mind as you listen to what your parents have to say. They are:

- *What do they mean; what are they trying to say?*

- *Why is it important to them?*

- *What important message could they be leaving out?*

General rules for listening

Relax, when you listen. This is important, because if you strain too hard, you are likely to find it harder to understand.

Hear your parents out

Wait and be patient before you start asking questions. Asking questions at the right time in a conversation often has the effect of helping your parents to more plainly say what they mean. If you listen to them, they will be more likely to further explain themselves. You will find that your parents will work harder in their efforts to get you to understand what they are trying to say.

- *Listen, without criticizing, passing judgment, or giving advice. Let your parents speak as freely and fully as possible without censure or blame.*

35

- *Restate what your parents have said, in a slightly different manner. This lets them know that you have listened and they are being understood.*

- *When your parents have finished speaking to you, accept what they have said. You can question what they have said if there is imminent danger to yourself or others, or some moral infraction or violation of a law.*

Use the "soft approach" if you need to disagree

- *Let them talk until they are finished.*

- *Avoid contradicting them.*

- *Stay focused on what they are saying.*

- *Listen attentively and carefully to what they say all the way through.*

- *Ask if they could look at it in a different way.*

- *Say, "You may be right, but would you be willing to consider...?"*

- *Say, "You may know more about this than I, but..."*

- *Say, "I realize you have a very good point, but can we look at it this way?"*

The "soft" and "gentle" approach will reduce your parents' resistance. This approach must be sincere and genuine. Sincerity can make the difference between acceptance and rejection of what is being conveyed. Mastering these techniques will allow more room for understanding and flexibility from all parties.

BODY LANGUAGE

Other than your appearance, communication is the most important impact you have on people. Approximately 70 to 80 percent of your life is spent communicating with others in a verbal or nonverbal way. Verbal expressions are those words that you actually speak. Nonverbal expressions are your own actions done in an obvious or subtle way. "Seeing is believing." Your body cannot tell a lie.

Unconsciously you tell what is going on in your mind by the way you walk, sit, hold your head, hands, and mouth, use your eyes, and position your legs and feet etc.

KINETICS

The science of "kinetics" is the study of physical movement of the body. If you want to find out what a person believes, watch what that person does. According to research, human beings give off approximately 700,000 nonverbal forms of communication. In communication, we always interact indirectly with people. Messages are constantly being sent and received during interactions with others, whether you know it or not. Be aware of the many kinds of nonverbal interactions.

THE PRIVATE ZONES

There is an area surrounding you which is considered an extension of your physical self. This is called your private or personal zone. When people invade this space, you have a tendency to perceive their actions as an invasion of your privacy. Sometimes, when people get too close to you, you may feel threatened, or at the least, their invasion makes you feel uncomfortable. People like about 2 1/2 to 3 feet of space between them and others in order to feel safe. You may become uneasy if people you don't know come closer than two or three feet.

Even if you have the best intentions, invading a person's private zone may cause him or her to feel uncomfortable. How you sit, stand, or recline can have a direct effect of the way you are perceived by others. You may be saying words of peace and calm, but, if your body position is perceived as challenging, you may be misunderstood.

NONVERBAL COMMUNICATION

Verbal expressions are only about 10 to 15 percent of the communication you deliver to others. The other 85 to 90 percent is interpreted from nonverbal cues. All you need to do is to alter your tone of voice, and your message will be relayed differently. Voice, tone, and body language become critical when you are asking for your parents' cooperation.

You must make a conscious effort to be selective in the words you use, position your body, and control your tone of voice. One of the best ways to monitor your communication is to watch how your parents respond by their facial and body expressions. Don't assume that people have gotten your message. Watch closely for their responses.

SEEING IS BELIEVING

People judge and evaluate you mostly by what they see. Opinions are quickly developed about who you are, after people see you and what you do. When you begin to speak, their opinions start to increase or decrease in a positive or negative way.

DRESS FOR SUCCESS/IMAGE BUILDING

Your appearance or the way you look is critical in setting the tone, or making a first impression. Remember, a human being gives off approximately 700,000 nonverbal signals. When you act, dress, or do something a certain way, you are communicating to others how you feel and what you believe. Most people receive your communication, but will not often let you know directly their impression of you. You have the ability to receive messages from others even though you cannot determine the exactness of what is being said.

10 Percent. 30 Percent. 60 Percent.

Consider the following when understanding communication. In a study conducted in the area of getting promoted or hired for a position, three factors were said to be most important. They are: *(1) education (2) politics (3) image.*

These three factors were given by people who are responsible for hiring and promotion within their companies. The study revealed some amazing results. The individuals who were in the position of selecting candidates indicated *education was only 10 percent* of their consideration. Education was considered to be important, but it was the least important of the three. You can expect every applicant to have the basic credentials, knowledge, skills, and experience for the type of occupation they are interested in. How you look to others, especially in the beginning, is what people consider most during the interaction.

Image was second to politics, with 30 percent of the consideration. Image is the way in which you are perceived by others. It is the way you look. Image is a vital part of managing. Your image can make it easier and better for those who wish to understand you and identify with you. It is the result of how you look, what you have done, or said to others.

These same individuals in the study identified *politics as 60 percent* of their consideration for hiring or promotion. Politics involves the people you know, the people who know you, and how well you get along with others. Getting along with others is a major key to your success as a human being, particularly regarding the relationship you have with mom and dad. How well you get along with others determines if you are a team player and if you're willing to reach out and understand others. There are some people who would say that *"everything you do is political."* Your politics with your parents will determine how you are perceived and whether you get what you want from them. Establish a good political position so it can work for you, and not against you. These three areas are definite communication considerations.

THE WAY YOU LOOK TO OTHERS

You have one opportunity to make a first impression when you meet people or when people are observing you. The way you are dressed can determine how people treat you. If you are dressed in dirty clothes when you walk into a fine restaurant, you may be informed by the staff that they have a dress code. Some restaurants have signs indicating how they want or expect for you to be dressed before entering their establishment.

MODESTY IS THE BEST WAY

In considering the way you dress study the way people interact with others. Learn what works so you can be successful. Look at the way people dress for weekly worship, interviews, dates, anniversaries, parties, or other occasions. What are they trying to do when they dress for these occasions? If you study the way they dress, you can conclude that these individuals are attempting to blend in, impress, or increase their chances of being accepted within a particular group.

Your selection of clothes, hairstyles, jewelry and make-up should appear modest. Generally, parents and other adults do not like extreme attire exemplifying some kind of rebellion. If a *modest approach* is remembered and used in almost every situation, you will make a very good first and future impression. Clothes, behaviors and styles that do not exceed the limits and are not excessive are considered modest. Who you really are should be clearly defined modestly through your image.

CONTROLLING WHAT YOU SAY

To become an effective communicator, you must become skilled in word usage in order to win arguments without making enemies and to make friends and be persuasive. These techniques require you to seek knowledge and sharpen the skills necessary to convey your message. How do you avoid arguing and becoming angry? By staying in control. From time to time, you will experience anger and frustrations which may cause you to become defensive or aggressive. How you handle your anger and frustration is very important, especially when it comes to your parents. Now is the time to realize that kindness, along with a cool, calm approach are what you are going to need to control yourself.

STAYING IN CONTROL

You can either react defensively or in a helpful manner if you are angered or frustrated by your parents. If your parents are angry or

40

frustrated, you can take advantage of these times to react in a helpful manner. Sometimes, your parents don't know how to react other than with anger or frustration in a particular situation. Take a deep breath. Use deep breathing techniques to calm and cool yourself down. Maintain a positive attitude, because being defensive or angry will not help the situation at all. It will only create more frustration. Reacting angrily opens you up for more disagreement and/or abuse. You can influence your parents' behavior and reaction by your behavior and reaction. If you are being treated with anger, chances are you are contributing to the anger by not knowing how to deal with it. Be kind and respectful. Listen and observe.

Be empathetic.

Empathy is making the effort to experience what someone feels before you pass judgment. Try to empathize with your parents when they are irate. Try to understand mom and dad's emotions and feelings. Then, try your best to figure out the remedy to the problem that has made them unhappy. You have to deal with both the emotion and the problem itself, before you can gain cooperation and agreement. The next time your parents get mad at you, remember, stay in control.

STAY COOL

There is no real reason for you to "blow your cool." Never allow your parents' reactions to place you on the defensive or cause you to become angry. Don't make excuses or blame others. Accept full responsibility, and you determine the outcome of the conversation. The incorrect thing to do would be to argue with your parents. If you make them look wrong, things will only get worse; and they will become even more irate. "Fighting fire with fire" usually means all parties get burned. Getting defensive is a guaranteed loss. Get on the offensive side by staying in control, being cool and positive.

MIRRORING

When you are listening to your parents, match their body language. If they sit down, you sit down next to them, slowly. If they stand up or walk away, you stand up slowly and walk with them in a non-aggressive manner. Keep a comfortable distance so their space will not be invaded. Look them in the eye with an expression of empathy and concern. Take the humble approach. React to their comments by saying *"yes ma'am/sir, I apologize. How can we resolve your concerns?"* If they get loud or disagreeable, calmly suggest moving into a more private area so you can listen to them. Stay calm. Don't take things personally.

LISTEN FOR THE FACTS

Listen for the facts. Angry parents will usually respond well, if they feel that you care about their feelings and problems. Treating their concerns in a casual way will only cause them to get even more angry.

Your parents demand to be heard. As you hear them out, listen for issues in which you can agree. Say, "I can see why you're upset and I want to help." This will show them you are sincere and do understand. In the end, most parents will calm down after you use this kind of approach. The next step is to find remedies to the problem as you continue to be caring towards them. If you have not determined the problem during the listening process, start asking questions; such as "Please tell me where I went wrong? How can I help...?"

Acknowledge you hear them by nodding your head.

Repeat their answers to them:

· *"So, you're saying..."*

· *"If I have this correct, you feel I..."*

OFFER SOLUTIONS

Once you have identified the problems and determined the remedies, offer your parents some good solutions or options. I cannot emphasize enough the importance of resolving problems positively. You need to let your mom and dad know what you can do, instead of what you cannot do. Be reliable and dependable when you have accepted the responsibility of resolving a problem. Be quick and prompt about it.

COMPLETE THE CONVERSATION AND FOLLOW UP

Be extra polite and courteous while doing what you can to improve the situation. Once you have taken care of their problems, ask if what you have done is "okay". And thank them. You may find this to be a little awkward for your parents who, just sometime before, were mad or upset with you. Keep in mind, you are managing your parents. Be very cooperative and supportive. Remember, it is only the angry, dissatisfied parent who may deny you what you want. When the time is right, contact them later in person or by telephone, to see if everything is okay. This simply places the "icing on the cake." It also shows that you really are concerned about their problems.

IT MAY NOT WORK 100 PERCENT OF THE TIME

Be aware that sometimes, it won't matter what you do to correct your parents' problems. But this is a rare occurrence. The majority of the time you are going to be successful in satisfying them and yourself. Sometimes, you may have parents who cannot be satisfied or just want to give you a hard time. If mom and dad are out of control, continue to say "yes ma'am/sir" and remain calm. You may tell them in a very diplomatic way that you are going to leave and come back later, if they will allow you to. If necessary, get another family member's assistance.

Dealing with parents who are upset and cannot calm down requires a lot of tact and sharpened skills. It is challenging for the best child. If you are often faced with these situations, find yourself an emotional outlet to relieve stress. Exercise or contact a professional counselor so you will have someone to talk to about your concerns. You are human too, and need consoling from time to time. Ask God to help you through those tough times.

BE A WINNER. BE NICE.

When you are able to use good communication skills, you develop a winning attitude. Parents will start to listen to you and advancements will come your way when you convince them to do what you want them to do.

When you meet your parents, select ahead of time a greeting that they will respond to positively. A greeting that will cause them to feel good right away. Hug them, hold their hands so they feel your sincerity. Right away, look for something you can compliment, such as their clothes, hair, general appearance, perfume or cologne, or a piece of jewelry. This technique is called *disarming*. It feeds into the person's ego. Do not be afraid to feed into a person's in the right way, especially when it comes to your parents. You want to concentrate on what you can do for your parents rather than what they can do for you. Every parent is an individual who has special needs, wants, and circumstances. The more you meet those needs the more you can get them on your side. You will soon learn that the more you give to the relationship the more you will get out of the relationship.

KNOW MOM AND DAD

Know your parents' basic desires. Be familiar with their lives and anticipate change. Understand their positions in life, in the community, and in their professions. Many children make the mistake of not considering their parents' status within their community, or with their profession. Many famous, loving and caring parents are embarrassed in the public's eye by the negative actions of their children. How often do we see a very progressive family grappling with the negativity of a relative, especially if it is their son or daughter.

Appreciate your parents' good reputation within the community, and do everything you can to support them by behaving positively. Be around people who are law-abiding, considerate of others, and who have their head on straight. Look out for your parents. Watch and listen for clues or hints that will enable you to understand them.

Listening to your parents raises their self-esteem. It feeds their ego. It helps them feel respected. It motivates them to want to talk with you verses to you. Listen attentively, with your eyes focused on theirs or on the center of their forehead. When they seem to lose interest and appear to be a little apprehensive, ask sincere and genuine questions relevant to the conversation. This will allow them to become more and more confident about talking. It is important that you talk to your parents as often as possible, so you can become more familiar with them.

STRAIGHT TALK

I want to mention one concern about speaking straight-to-the point and probing your parents. In some instances, truth can hurt. Nowadays, parents are prying and probing their children about issues that were barely discussed when they were young. Today's openness with parents is fueled by other circumstances, as well. Many of today's parents grew up in the 50s', 60s' and 70s', a time when it was popular to promote honesty as the best policy. But, with each passing day and with new social developments, being open is even more delicate.

You may be placed in an awkward position with your attempts to be honest and straight forward. You must be aware of parents who become easily offended or hurt when it comes to candor.

BE TACTFUL

Tact, sensitivity and empathy are skills you must master. Parents may want to probe or pry into your personal life. Your parents may want to know if you have ever tried drugs, have ever had sex, or when you lost your virginity. These questions can be embarrassing for you and them. Think carefully about their questions before answering. You may want to tell them that their questions are too personal and you feel uncomfortable discussing your private matters. You may also be tempted to ask them the same kinds of questions. Be careful your parents do not hear private conversations that are not meant for them to hear. Of course, balancing between "talking straight " and the need for privacy may be challenging. Prepare yourself for this challenge.

PART 6

MANAGING

WHAT IS A MANAGER?

The next step in managing your parents is understanding what a manager does and what management is. A *manager* is one who utilizes available resources to accomplish a task. A manager works with and through people. A manager provides the starting point for the relationship. A manager is the person formally in charge of the expectations. A manager is a person who gets the job done by reaching goals and accomplishing tasks with the tools, equipment, people, money, supplies, etc., that he or she has at his/her disposal.

WE ARE ALL BORN MANAGERS!

Contrary to the opinion that managers are made, I believe everyone is born a manager and given resources to use to get what he/she wants, or to get a job done. Some people think that managers are developed to do a certain job. People can be trained to recognize, develop and refine their management skills, but all the tools to be a manager are given to you when you are born. You soon become aware of the resources you have through attempts to achieve what you want. Through a process of trial and error, you learn what works and what doesn't. Your parents can bring out the best in you as you develop and refine your skills. Like any skill, management skills get better with practice.

HOW TO BEGIN MANAGING?

The best way to start managing is to learn all you can about your parents. Get to know who they are as people. I hear mothers and fathers express a need to show more attention to their children. Usually, children expect their parents to give all the attention, support, love and care. As a manager, you will do just the opposite. Stop depending on your parents for attention, and give them your attention. The more you give them the more you will receive in return.

When you give attention to your parents, you will reap what you sow. One of the best ways to get positive attention is to give it.

KNOW THEIR BACKGROUND

- *Where and when they were born.*

- *Their life experiences and education.*

- *Their habits.*

- *Their attitude about work.*

- *Their ambitions.*

- *Their family and social life, and so on.*

KNOWLEDGE IS POWER, IF YOU REMEMBER TO USE IT

This information is essential because you need to have a good idea about how your parents will react in a given situation or how they will respond to you. You must be very tactful and diplomatic in acquiring this information from your parents. Learn when and how to ask questions, and when to listen.

ROLES OF A MANAGER

A manager has many duties and responsibilities. There are certain roles you will play that will have a big impact on managing your parents. What are the roles of a manager? How do they play a part in managing your parents? Managerial roles can be identified in several areas. Listed are the most important ones:

- *The manager as a leader*

- *The manager's interpersonal role*

- *The manager's informational role*

- *The manager's liaison role*

- *The manager as a monitor*

- *The manager as a disseminator*

- *The manager's decision making role*

- *The change manager*

- *The manager as a disturbance handler*

- *The manager as a negotiator*

SHARPEN YOUR SKILLS

You will utilize one or more of these roles in managing your parents and while the roles are described individually, they cannot be separated. All of the roles make up a *complete manager.* You cannot delete one role and expect the other roles to remain completely functional. For instance, if you stop being a liaison, you may lose access to outside information that can help your condition. This could also prohibit you from serving as the link between other family members in disputes and or negotiations. This will decrease your ability to pass on information as a disseminator, which will directly impact your decision making, which will affect your leadership and so on. Your challenge is to sharpen the skills required in each of these roles.

When opportunity meets desire, when the circumstances exist and you want to do something about them, you will be able to employ the skills relevant to these roles.

MANAGER'S ROLES EXPLAINED

A manager as a leader - A leader is a person who is moving in a

48

direction and can convince others to follow his/her vision in a positive or negative way. Leaders are born and made to become "better" leaders. You are a leader! Norman Vincent Peale once said, "Nothing is more confusing than people who give advice but set bad examples." You must lead with your actions, because actions speak louder than words.

Characteristics of a good leader.

- *A leader has internal control and takes full responsibility for their decisions and actions.*

- *A leader sees his/her purpose as one of working together rather than controlling or manipulating others.*

- *A leader is concerned about others and sensitive to others' needs and feelings.*

- *A leader is a goal achieving individual.*

- *A leader is willing to share feelings and thoughts with others they trust.*

Everything you do is screened by others who are searching for leadership. When managing your parents, you must become a leader not only for yourself, but for your parents, sisters, brothers and other relatives. Leadership is a critical role for any manager. Leaders lead by example. So be a good example. The leadership role is the most significant. It permeates all management roles. Each time you encourage your parents, you are acting as leaders. As your managing power manifests itself, you will begin to realize the positive contributions you can make!

The Manager as Spokesperson

The manager may have to lead by speaking on behalf of the family's relationship. This can occur by request from someone else or when you recognize the need, based on certain factors. To perform this role, you must deliver accurate information at all times. One of the most important things to remember about this role is the truth and speaking straight-to-the-point when communicating with your parents.

The interpersonal roles of a manager - The main purpose of the interpersonal role is to manifest positive power within the relationship between individuals. Power, in this sense, is to be used in a positive way to better the relationship. These are some of the interpersonal skills you must develop for the relationship:

· *Diplomacy.*
· *Winning an argument without making an enemy.*
· *Winning friends and influencing people.*
· *Being polite and courteous.*

The informational roles - You live in a world of information. Information leads you to knowledge. Knowledge is power, if you remember to use it. Information is an important key in any relationship. Staying in touch and keeping your parents advised is very important. If you fail to give them information, they will not know if you have done something outstanding, or what was expected of you. Do not wait until something goes wrong in the relationship before you let them know what is actually going on. Inform them of all positive achievements in your life, no matter how large or small. If you do not live with your parents, call them at least once a day just to say "hello". By all means, stay in touch and let them know their well-being is important to you. Providing information to your parents will improve your image. The more your parents know about your willingness to improve the relationship, the more they will value you.

Informing your parents allows them to feel that they are making an impact on your life. Let your parents know ways they can contact you if they need anything. Every parent wants to know how their child is doing, and the more you inform them the better you are perceived. Getting, sharing and understanding information is essential.

The manager as a liaison - The leadership role stresses authority and power. The liaison role involves building and maintaining the significant web of mutually beneficial external relationships.

For example:

- *You may join outside groups or organizations, or attend seminars, workshops, conferences, or conventions to let your parents know that you are continuing your education. This will help them to know that you are the kind of person who makes decisions based on knowledge rather than impulse.*

- *You may join committees in your community or work-related environment, all of which provide contacts which will produce information and favors for you. This lets your parents know that if they need anything from an outside source, you are their contact.*

- *You can act as the go-between for a family member and your parents. This function is very important, especially if there is conflict between another relative and your parents. You can also assist your parents if they are having problems with products they may have purchased from a store. You can run the interference for them by contacting customer service from that store and negotiating a good solution for both parties. In this role, you become the bridge between your parents, other people, and outside concerns.*

The manager as monitor - As a monitor, you are always seeking information and understanding any circumstances concerning your parents' needs. Your role will be to constantly observe what is taking place within the relationship as well as what is going on in the environment.

The observations will clearly indicate that you are receiving a wide variety of information from a wide variety of sources. This will occur both inside and outside of the relationship. Get constant feedback. Look at the relationship through your parents' eyes. Think about how these questions apply to you:

Are you asking questions?

Are you paying attention to details?

Do you have a strategy in place for improving conditions?

Are you using the information you receive?

Are you asking your parents to give you a verbal rating on how you are doing with the relationship?

Ask, "How am I doing?" or "How can I become better?" You need to know what is going on in the relationship and also know how it became that way.

Consider how a coach and a player get along. Place yourself in both of these positions. Let your parents play the role of the score keeper. You are the player and the coach. The player and coach know more about what is going on than the score keeper. You are your best source for knowing what is going on in the relationship. You manage your parents everyday and have the best insight on why conditions are the way that they are, as well as how you can improve them. Ask yourself these questions:

What is the biggest ongoing concern I face with managing my parents?

If I were the parent and could make at least one change, what would it be?

In this role, you must become an "opportunity spotter" looking behind and in front of you so that the relationship is protected.

The manager as a disseminator - Because of the access to information and resources that a manager has, they are able to play the role of disseminator. Relaying information inside or outside of the relationship from one person to another, is a vital function. Getting information and resources, and sharing them in a timely fashion is important. You are the one who has to inform your parents of any upcoming events so there won't be any surprises. School proms, graduation ceremonies, meetings, appointments, special occasions, birthdays, pregnancies, relevant news, SAT schedules, and bills they may have to pay, are just some of the many things that mom and dad need to know. It is your responsibility to keep them informed.

The decision-making role - Successful managers are clear-minded individuals. Their positions require them to make difficult decisions and take calculated risks. "The buck stops" with the manager when his/her decisions are made. Managers can make quick decisions when they need to be made. They can make important decisions without acting prematurely. They can also remember to make decisions without being reminded. A manager thinks before he or she acts. This role involves the manager's strategy-making process. As a manager, you must develop the ability to make decisions in a rapidly changing world. A manager is constantly making decisions for the betterment of the relationship. The bottom line is, make a decision when a decision needs to be made.

The change manager - The key is to manage change by recognizing and understanding what the impact of the change will be. It is said. "A wise man changes often, fools rarely change." Change is a fact of life. There is nothing more permanent than change. Today, new innovations and techniques are being developed to carry us into the 21st century. The way we live, the way we think, the way we are currently doing things causes us to change.

Change is constant. Social, economic, political, and religious changes are occurring in the world. Go to the grocery store. Visit a movie theater. Take your parents to a baseball game. You will find prices are changing, as are the way in which you are served, and the quality of the products. Vending machines are replacing the "personal touch" we used to enjoy.

And, of course, the people in these kinds of business are changing, also. During the 60s', much emphasis was placed on automation. According to the predictions at that time machines would do the work that were previously being done by humans. And, those who had not prepared for the age of automation would be left without jobs and pay to support themselves.

CHANGE, BIGGER THAN EXPECTED

Those people who forecasted change during the 60s' era described what they saw as automation. I think the predictions of automation fell short of what we are actually experiencing today. It is not automation that has taken the world by storm, but computerization and the ability to access information. The buzz word is now "high tech".

There is a song that says, "Everything must change, nothing remains the same..." As a human being, you are constantly changing. Your mind never holds the same thoughts from one moment to next.

Your body is constantly creating new cells, and old cells are dying. So, everything must change and will change. The questions you should ask are, "How do you prepare for change?" "How do you manage change?" And, "How can you recommend and receive change?" Before you answer any of these questions, understand that change must occur first from within. You cannot expect others to change before you change yourself from within. You cannot expect your condition to change, unless you make a decision to change. The Qur'an says that *"God does not change a condition of a people unless they change themselves..."*

MANAGING CHANGE

Change can present new challenges for you. People are afraid to change for various reasons. Some fear losing control of their current situations. Others fear the inclusion of other people in the decision making. Also, the unknown outcome of the change causes most people to resist. Now that you have made a decision to manage your parents, they will begin to realize a change in you. You will have to assist them during this transition so they won't be too surprised.

Your parents may doubt your sincerity, but let them know about your desire to better your relationship with them, including some of the changes they can expect from you. This will reduce their resistance towards the changes made in your relationship.

There are relationships that will succeed under the circumstances of change and some that will fail. Why? Why are some people more successful than others when it comes to managing change? It's because successful people who manage change are aware and attentive to change.

Major changes have occurred within the past 35 years which have had a direct impact on parents and children. During the late 60s', when the "generation gap" was a main focus, many family relationships became strained. In the 70s' and 80s', the constant stream of women entering the job market was a drastic change. Women were now spending more time in their careers than at home. According to the 1992 US Department of Labor figures, women will account for 62 percent of the labor force growth from now until the year 2005. About 67 percent of the 34 million women who are mothers with children under 18 years-old hold jobs. Today, women command 46 percent of the job market.

CHANGE BRINGS OPPORTUNITY FOR GROWTH

Always think of new ways to manage change. How can you become a good *change manager?* Start by being perceptive of your circumstances, surroundings and environment. Notice more! Look, and examine the things that are happening around you. Be hungry with curiosity and ask questions. Be open-minded. Be flexible, and demonstrate a high willingness to learn. Be willing to adapt to new, faster, more efficient and better ways. If one managing technique doesn't work for you, change your approach and try another.

Become optimistic and enthusiastic. Act on optimism and think of ways to help your parents experience the least resistance to change. Encourage them not to worry about the changing economy. If the country is experiencing inflation, tell mom and dad that inflation allows you to utilize your resources a lot better. When situations in your family are dismal, find a way to look at the brighter side of things.

When your parents seem to express gloom or pessimism about a particular matter, show them the challenge can have a favorable outcome. A "change manager" is an "opportunity spotter". Change can be difficult for your parents. When difficulty exists, take the opportunity to help your parents grow. Turn problems into opportunities of progress. Try to become a "trend setter" by understanding and taking the initiative to manage change. When change occurs within your family, take the lead to carry the family in a better direction. You can make a good impression on your brothers, sisters, or other relatives by setting the tone.

Changing Times - Today, a large number of companies are cutting the workforce and reassessing their ways of doing business. Many companies that were prosperous years ago are now out of business, because they did not recognize change until it was too late. As a result, employees bore the consequences of not preparing for the possibility of being laid off. Maybe your parents did as well. Why? Because sometimes people do not anticipate change. I believe employees should become proactive by helping their companies recognize change and suggesting better ways of management so jobs can be maintained. Suggest the same proposals to your parents so they may be prepared for possible future lay-offs.

Develop an *"early detection system"* to identifying areas where change may occur. Get with others who are perceptive to change. Listen to your intuition. Master being an *opportunity spotter,* by practicing and sharpening your skills in order to manage change.

REDUCING THE RESISTANCE TO CHANGE

Develop a strategy for each change to reduce the resistance in the relationship. If a change is to occur, the person or persons who are going to be affected by the change should be informed in advance, if at all possible, and given an opportunity for some constructive input. This will reduce the resistance to change. Get your parents involved when change is anticipated, or occurs. Parents need to have a way of expressing their feelings about a given situation that may mean change for them.

Modifying your goals, objectives and strategies may be necessary in helping them deal with change. Your parents can accept change, if they believe that they have some say concerning their future.

The manager as a disturbance handler - The ability to handle crises or disturbances is an essential skill you must have. The word "crisis" comes from the Greek word "krsis" which means to decide or sift. The most often usage of the word "crisis" is a time of emotional and personal turmoil, or disturbance for many people. Disturbances in one's life can lead to serious and far-reaching consequences.

During life's disturbances, there may be dangers, fears or precarious situations. Disturbances or crises are times for caution but also times of growth and improvement. Disturbances can be great opportunities. People whose lives are being disturbed, are people who are open for change more so than most people under ordinary circumstances. Parents may be experiencing loss or change within their careers, their relationships with their spouses, their health, finances, and so on. If these conditions are not recognized and dealt with effectively, they can escalate and become worse. The heightened and escalated emotional level of a parent makes rational communication challenging. When you are in control of your circumstances, it's easier to be rational. You hear words, see their logic, and react accordingly. However, when you become disturbed, threatened, fearful, or stressed, rational communication takes a back seat to lower levels of communication. Lower levels of communication disregard rationality. Instead, it focuses on body language and tone of voice.

When parents and children experience disturbances in their lives, communication suffers. Remember, what frustrated, stressed parents may need most is to free themselves through expression. Helping them during their disturbances develops closeness. Most people show some indication that disturbance is building up. If you can detect the build-up early on, a supportive, empathetic approach can usually resolve the condition. The thing to remember is people, in the early stages of disturbances, will show signs of losing control or being irrational.

This is a major reason why you, as a disturbance handler, must have good skills. You can be very effective for your parents when they are experiencing disturbances in their lives. In this case, positive communication may be the best opportunity towards helping them make significant improvements in their lives and in their relationships.

Disturbance handler skills, when acquired, can be refined to be even more effective. All unexpected or anticipated disturbances or crises should be handled with a calm approach. If your parents experience a crisis or disturbance in their lives, it will probably have a negative impact on the relationship you have with them. They may become resistant to your attempts to help them, and become a non-cooperative. There are reasons commonly known to cause non-co-operation and resistance. They are frustration, seeking attention, and testing authority. Non-cooperation and resistance to your management strategies can be disturbing for all parties. Sometimes, your parents may resist you because of frustration from dealing with your past actions. Your parents have been dealing with you, family members, along with other things all their lives. Dealing with such a load can be difficult and also frustrating for them. They may seek or need your attention when they are disturbed and frustrated by problems. Parents can test your ability to handle their frustration, and seek your attention to help them find a solution. Be willing to manage their disturbances.

Another opportunity you may have in managing disturbances is when mom and dad are dealing with your brothers and sisters. You may have known of situations when mom and dad have had to confront your brothers or sisters involving some family matter. When you and other relatives disregard your parents' instructions, agreement on any solution or compliance may not seem possible. Arguing can become intense.

Be the liaison. Step in and calmly handle their disturbance. Seize the opportunity to give positive solutions and assist your mother and father by showing leadership skills. Your parents will certainly appreciate you for this if you can help keep your brothers and sisters in line.

The manager as a negotiator - Negotiating is a skill that is critical to managing your parents. It is said, "Ask and you shall receive... Seek and you will find..." Negotiation is nothing more than seeking by asking for the things you want in a diplomatic and tactful way. It is an art. It can be refined to the point that you can become an effective negotiator. You are always negotiating by interaction when you are talking to your parents and others. Over a period of time, you may discuss receiving permission or seeking your parents' or others' approval for getting what you want. This is negotiation. Negotiating skills are not just for the union leader, police officer, or FBI agent, they are for you. And, if you know how to structure the conversation and interact, you will get what you want from your parents and others. Effective negotiating will remove the pressure and stress in the relationship, if done properly.

If you are a minor, most of everything you want is controlled by your parents. If you live with your parents, they can tell you when to come and go. They may control the food you eat, the visitors you can have, the clothes you wear and telephone usage. Your parents control a number of significant things in your life that often contribute to the development of your self-concept, image, and self-esteem. Now, doesn't it make sense for you to spend the necessary time learning how to get what you want? By learning these basic skills of negotiation, you will able to get what you want, without controlling, manipulating, or dominating your parents.

You want to develop a style where you are not turning your parents off, but turning them on so they can help you. When you ask your parents for their permission, approval, or anything you may want, this is called *presenting your proposal.* In submitting your proposal, which does not have to be in writing, you are requesting that your parents take a look at what you want in order that they give you a favorable response.

Know, with negotiation, there are predictable responses, especially when it comes to mom and dad. If you ask your parents for permission or for a favor, they may:

· *Reject your proposal outright*
. *Say "yes" to the first request*
. *Not give an answer, until they consider it further*

When looking at these predictable responses, you stand a pretty good chance of negotiating a favorable outcome on behalf of all parties if you know what to do next. What should you do when these responses are given? You should remember not to take their responses personal if they appear negative. Use their outright rejections and unavailable responses as an opportunity to negotiate by getting them to say "yes" to your proposals. You become a good negotiator when you are concerned about your parents getting what they want as well as you getting what you want.

In negotiating with your parents, understand that they may not want the same things you want. You may assume that what is important to you, is also important to them. This may not be true. You see things one way and your parents see things another way. This assumption can never lead to a win-win outcome until you recognize they may not want the same things in the negotiation. If you were to show your parents a picture and ask them what they saw in that picture, it would probably be different than what you saw. It is absolutely okay for your parents to see things differently in any situation concerning your proposal.

There are three phases of negotiation and if you learn these three phases and how to work with them, you can become very effective and exceed even your own expectations.

The first phase is:

> *Gather all of the information you can get on your proposal or condition. Find out how your parents regard considering your proposal.*

The second phase is:

> *Find out what your parents intend to do about your proposal. Ask questions and probe.*

The third phase is:

> *Find areas of compromise. Be willing to give something in order to get something in return. You are not looking to make a deal, but rather, to give a service to your parents.*

You must be a firm believer in a win-win negotiation instead of dominating, outsmarting or tricking your parents into getting or doing something for you which they would not normally do. You should be able to discuss or work out your concerns in order to get what you want. Take for instance, your allowance, the amount of money your parents give to you if you have taken care of weekly or monthly responsibilities. You may want to receive more than what has traditionally been given to you and your parents may want to continue the original amount. Your parents control the money. So, how can you and your parents win? Remember, it is okay for them to feel differently than you.

Don't assume that money is the most important thing to your parents. It could be they want you to learn the value of earning more money, by doing more for the dollar. It could be they may think you are going to waste additional money on unwanted items or unnecessary things.

If you ask for something, such as more allowance, and your parents reject your proposal or question it, remember the three phases of the negotiation and put them to use. At this time of their rejection or inquiry, you should simply agree with their concerns. Do not argue with your parents. Try to always agree with them. Arguing forces them to defend their position. Agreeing with them defuses their competitive position. If you find yourself arguing with your parents, it is because you are not thinking. Say, "You are right. I agree. I understand your concerns." This will be the point where you gradually turn things around in your favor. Be humble.

Do not be a competitive threat when negotiating. *Consider how dogs act in their natural environment. If a dog is unable to defend himself and is aggressed by another dog who is stronger; the weaker dog often times rolls on its back, open its legs, exposes its throat, and submit to the stronger dog's aggression. Then the stronger dog usually growls and hisses, but will not harm the weaker dog. And eventually, the strong dog will leave the weaker one alone. If the weaker dog is not aware of his position and his strengths, and goes on to compete or challenge the stronger dog, you can just imagine what would happen. The weaker dog will only get chewed up in the process.* So is it when you are arguing with your parents. If you argue, compete, or challenge them, more than likely, you are going to lose the argument and make matters worse.

For example, if you request your parents' permission to go out for the weekend to attend an activity, they may say no. Say, "I agree with you." They will probably look at you in amazement and say, "You do?" You will reply, "Sure." This is a time where you would have done your homework and know more about your proposal and the issue of parental permission. You may want to say that:

Most parents interviewed in a recent study say they prefer not to give their children permission to go out on the weekend. When questioned further, these same parents agreed that the weekend is the only time that is truly available for their children to relax and enjoy themselves.

Remind them of this by saying, "And, you do want me to have a little enjoyment don't you? I can leave and return at a decent time. I assure you that I will be on my best conduct and use good judgment while I am out."

In this situation, you must have your negotiation strategy planned in advance. If you know you want to go out for the weekend, make sure you set goals for the negotiation and implementation of your strategy at the time of the discussion. Offer a reciprocal favor, such as "I will clean up my room for one month straight and improve my grades in schools if you will consider my proposal." If they say no, be very diplomatic and say, "I understand." Ask if there is something else that may be of concern.

When they tell you what their concern is, remember to agree, but say, *"can we look at this another way?"* and offer another concession. Timing is important, but be tactful when negotiating. Know when to agree. Let the conversation simmer down and come back later with another reciprocal offer. Once you come to an agreement, shake their hands or hug them for a win-win outcome.

There is more to negotiation than you can get from these examples. Remember though, that negotiation is always a two-way street. You want something and your parents want something. Have the desire to acquire the skills of negotiating and understanding, and practice your skills. Practice whenever you get a chance.

Remember your roles as a manager are definite keys to a successful relationship with mom and dad. Practice each one and put them to use right away.

PART 7

UNDERSTANDING YOUR PARENTS

IDENTIFYING BEHAVIORS

You may be wondering why your parents react in a positive or negative way. Well, aside from whatever stress they may be experiencing, they may be a bit envious of you. Lets examine a few reasons:

- *You are younger, firmer, stronger and more energetic.*

- *You have your whole life ahead of you.*

- *You are having a lot of fun and enjoying more freedom.*

- *You may be able to enjoy a better career and financial opportunities.*

- *Your romantic life may appear more interesting.*

- *You can physically do things they may not be able to do.*

Oftentimes, you tend to give more attention to other people or things than to your parents. As your mom and dad both know, the job of raising you does not end when you reach age 18. You will probably spend more time in college, delay marriage, and may have problems finding a job during unfriendly economic times. Your challenges, as a result, add more years of parental responsibility. According to a 1993 US Census Bureau report

"More than five million children between the ages of 25 and 34 lived at home with their parents in 1993, compared to two million children who did in 1970."

In fact, living with your parents longer, as they watch you prosper, creates complex feelings in them. Now is a precarious time for you and your parents. Your parents may feel that you are living in a more dangerous time than they did, because you are being exposed to more. They, on the other hand, were not given chances to do some of the things you are doing now.

~~At the same time, you are demanding the opportunity to control~~ your own life and be given your own right to grow up. Therefore, you have to take into consideration that subconsciously they may be feeling insecure, lonely, and afraid.

LIFE AFTER 30

Ask anyone who is over thirty years old how fast life tends to go by. Your parents may feel their lives are rapidly coming to an end. You should do things to reassure them that now is their best time! Being the best they can be is what's important, and you are here to help them.

PARENTS HAVE A VISION

There are going to be times when your parents will insist and demand that you achieve in order to be successful. These are their most sincere attempts to help you. They really care for you. Most of the time, your parents love you more than you care and love yourself. They are looking to your future whereas you may often make decisions just for the moment. They see what the consequences could be if you made certain decisions. Remember, these are the individuals who have had many years of experience and acquired much knowledge you may never fully appreciate.

Please understand when mom or dad make a decision or ask you to do something, they are protecting their investment - you. They mean well and have good intentions. They love you. They may simply lack much needed opportunities or know-how to express their appreciation. When they see "working together" works, they are going to be in favor of it. Working together will provide opportunities for their positive appreciation.

Think about how your parents were brought up. Most of them grew up in an autocratic environment. The kind that says, "Do what I say do, and no back-talk." When you start managing your parents, you are asking them to change by allowing you to become a full partner in the relationship. This is breaking a cycle. They may fear your efforts and can become uneasy with the new arrangements. Demonstrate that you are willing to change, instead of asking them to.

You can never change your parents by getting mad, pouting, or openly disagreeing with them. Treat your parents the way they are and not by the way you are. You do not have to agree with them, just accept them and their ways unconditionally.

MOM AND DAD ARE A "TEAM"

If you have a good relationship with one parent and not with the other, do as much as possible to correct this situation. Recognize, these individuals often work together. They are a *team.* They have been doing things together for a very long time as a team. Establish a good rapport with the parent you do not communicate with well, in a sincere and genuine way. Realize, they know each other's likes and dislikes. They spend a great deal of valuable time together. Your mom and dad pretty much understand each other a lot better than you do and they were together, in most cases, before you ever came into the picture. Their first obligation or priority within the family is to each other. They must help and support each other before they can help and support you. Your parents must always appear to be united in their thinking and in their decision making. Help keep both parents in agreement on family matters. Never do anything that will create a conflict between them. Never contradict your parents, or do things which will cause them to disagree with one another. Promote harmony between your parents.

Be careful not to disregard one parent's decision over the other. For example, if you wanted to borrow money from your mother, and you asked her for a loan, it might happen that she may not be able to lend you any money. Do not go to your father and ask for a loan, afterward. Instead, think before you ask and remember mom and dad need to make the decision together if you are seeking their help.

Always try to speak to both parents at the same time, whenever possible, about important matters. This will show respect toward both parents, and it will allow them to make a decision as a team. If one parent is unavailable, ask the one who is available to share your concerns with the absent one. This helps them stay in harmony with one another.

Don't pressure them. Allow them to make decisions together by giving them a chance to think. This means you must plan your life and circumstances so they will not have to adjust to you. This will minimize interference in their plans. Recognize the importance of getting both of your parents' support for a favorable decision.

PARENT CLASSIFICATIONS

Parenting styles can be classified many different ways. One common distinction focuses on the element of authority or leadership involving the parent and child. According to this classification, parents *may be autocratic, democratic,* or *laissez-faire.*

What are autocratic parents?

Autocratic parents emphasize commands and order giving. Such parents make most of the important decisions, while entrusting little decision-making to you. These parents stand out clearly as "the boss," and there is little difficulty identifying them. Children may "shake in their shoes" when these individuals arrive unexpectedly. They may become nervous in response to a call from this type of parents. These parents utilize negative reprimands and reinforcements to develop a sense of fear in their children. Very strict rules are usually in place in order to maintain desired discipline from their children. These parents tell their children what to do and how to do it. They expect for the instructions to be adhered to or carried out immediately.

What is a democratic parent?

In contrast to autocratic parents, *democratic* parents show greater deference toward their children. Rather than constantly telling them what to do, they consult them. Their children's ideas and suggestions are valued. Some democratic parents even discuss financial problems as a family issue. They may view a proposed solution by any one of the family members as a desired way to solving the prob-

66

lem. Such an approach is often characterized by "family meetings." A family meeting allows you to discuss concerns and have some input by giving suggestions or solutions.

Democratic parents play an active role in stimulating the family's thinking towards developing solutions to a particular problem. Positive reinforcement, more freedom, and increased rewards are the results of these efforts.

What is a laissez-faire parent?

Laissez-faire parents are "free reign parents." They turn most of the decisions over to their children. Children determine their own rules and disciplines. They have to deal with their own problems, and often have no guidance or structure. This approach is characterized by the absence of leadership from the parents. These parents accept very little responsibility for their children's decision making. Although laissez-faire parents may experience a few successes from their children, chaos and confusion may result also from this kind of leadership.

AGING, INJURED OR SICK PARENTS

Adult children are faced with their parents aging, dying and, in some cases, their physical disabilities. You may find yourself making life-and-death medical decisions for them. These are challenges you will have to face sooner or later. My grandmother said, *"if you live long enough, you will get old."* And if you live long enough, someone will have to help take care of you. I have watched both of my grandparents age, develop health problems, and pass away. My grandfather lived until his 70s. My grandmother was 106 years old when she passed away. My father aged and developed conditions which contributed to his declining health and eventual death. I have watched my mother age over the years and observed the challenges she has faced. I have seen how their lives changed because of the aging process, including the stress it brought into their lives.

SILENCE IS WISDOM

As they aged, I noticed my relatives complaining and becoming more stubborn. Fortunately, I remembered what these individuals had done for me all of my life. I remembered to respect them and remain patient and silent in some instances. I simply kept my mouth shut, replied "yes sir or ma'am", and listened to them. These individuals also seemed to find the need to talk more and be heard. I made a commitment to find time for them during their time of need.

I also find myself calling or visiting my mother and my aging relatives more. I realize that I am going to need to assist them with some of their business or personal matters. On some occasions, my wife and I find ourselves going to the store, the pharmacy, the hospital or other places for them and with them, because they cannot get around on their own as safely. You may feel awkward or shy about befriending your parents and relatives during these times. Their conditions may not be what you are used to dealing with.

Here are some ways to help:

- *Get information on aging, death and managing disabilities.*

- *Visit or stay in touch with your parents on a regular basis.*

- *Schedule time for them.*

- *Give them a number where you can be reached in case of emergencies.*

- *Obtain their physician's number. Know where to locate their insurance papers.*

- *Be proactive, think and do some of the things that are positive ahead of time, without being asked or told.*

- *Treat them well.*

KNOW WHEN TO TALK TO THEM

It's okay to ask mom and dad how they are doing, or about their disabilities. It is also okay for them to talk about their disabilities. It is okay for you to offer your help or assistance. But ask first or wait until you are asked. When you talk to your parents, sit down next to them so that they feel equal or close to you. Invite your brothers, sisters, or other relatives on visits to your parents' home. The more relatives you can get involved to provide companionship for your parents, the better. Think about ways you can include them in what you do, such as family activities.

Remember the saying, "Once an adult, twice a child." You will one day become childlike in your old age and need the assistance or help of others. So *"Do unto others as you would have others to do unto you."*

THE THREE R's:
REBELLION RESENTMENT RETALIATION.

If the parent/child relationship is not good, the first sign of trouble is *rebellion.* A child usually starts to rebel against instructions and authority around 13 years old. Sometimes, it may continue until adulthood if the child does not correct himself or herself. Your parents can also become rebellious and resentful as they age. They may feel that they are in absolute authority when it comes to your life. So, why should they have to cooperate with you at all?

Eventually, if the rebellious stage is not recognized and dealt with effectively, *resentment* will set in. Dislike may contribute to the breakdown of the total relationship. This could develop into physical aggression or *retaliation,* if not corrected. The desire to "get even" and seek revenge manifests itself through destructive behavior. Verbal, and sometimes physical, abuse and punishment can be inflicted by you or your parents. A recent case in California showed the extent to which the relationship between parents and their sons regressed to the point of retaliation. The sons in the case actually killed their parents as a result of years of resentment, and the desire to get even. This was an extreme case. You, more than likely, will correct yourself long before these feelings occur. Be aware if your relationship has regressed to this level, and do everything you can to correct the situation.

Most negative relationships do not regress to the point of physical destruction of another person. However, individuals who are in this kind of predicament find verbal ways to destroy each other.

DIFFICULT PARENTS

What about so-called "difficult parents?" This situation can be challenging, but not impossible to overcome. If your parents overburden you with too much work and unrealistic expectations, sharpen your manager skills even more. Refer to the sections on communication and being proactive. Your skills, patience, and perseverance will be tested. Identify solutions for the challenge. Make sure your parents appreciate your good deeds.

You may have stubborn parents. When you make a request, they may immediately come up with several excuses to say no. When this occurs, try noticing one or two things. They may be letting you know their real reason why they are objecting to your request, or they may be playing *hard to convince.* When this happens, do not take their attitude personally. Be proactive when they need convincing. You can ask them to let you know if their objection is the "real reason" so that you can address their concerns. They will give you their true feelings only if you ask them to let you know if they have other reasons for denying you approval.

Changes in demographics, economics, and values have all led to mom and dad's stress. How are your parents being challenged? To understand what your parents are experiencing on a daily basis is to know and understand stress.

STRESS

Stress is necessary to life and cannot be avoided. The Qur'an says, *"Surely we created man for toil and struggle..."* The Bible discusses *"trials and tribulations."* Trials and tribulations, toils and struggles are conditions of stress. In fact, without stress, we cannot survive or grow as human beings. Warith Deen Muhammad said, *"A life of resistlessness is a life of death."* The only time you are in a tension free mode is when you are asleep, or dead. So it's important to know how to manage stress because the only time stress becomes negative is when it cannot be managed effectively.

DIVORCE

Divorced parents sometimes have difficulty managing the stress brought on by the break-up of the relationship. For those children whose parents are divorced, or are in the process of divorcing, be aware of their situation and do not add unnecessary stress. It is not your fault that they are divorced or divorcing. Don't blame yourself for the breakup. They will always be your parents. Try to be considerate and kind. Unrealistic expectations also create stress. Don't compare your parents to anyone else. They are their own people.

YOU FEEL THEIR STRESS

Research has shown that even babies can sense tension by the way their parents hold them or talk to them. And even now, you can recognize when they are under stress by paying attention to their nonverbal communication.

Parents may be the last people to recognize stress, because they do not openly talk about it. As a result, mom and dad may unknowingly add to their already stressful condition by becoming angry over simple matters. You don't want to add to their stress. *You want your interaction with them to be "stress relieving" and pleasing.* Your interaction with them can be a time when you do more for them. Sometimes, *mom and dad are so busy trying to be good parents they often neglect to give themselves the time they need for themselves.*

Rushing to spend quality time with you during the weekend, after they have had a week on the job, often causes them to forget about investing quality time in themselves. This condition creates more tension and becomes even more counterproductive for everyone.

71

RECOGNIZING AND MANAGING STRESS

To relieve stress, involve yourself in some form of physical exercise. According to research, exercise is the number one stress reliever. Exercising allows you to burn off steam and frustration, in addition to realigning your systems. Get involved in hobbies. Try a different approach by getting counseling in stress management and sharing this information with your parents.

PART 8

STRATEGIES FOR MANAGING

Every situation is different and a strategy that works in one family may not work in yours. Learn from you mistakes. Keep trying. Never give up. Accomplish your goals, even if people are opposing you and obstacles are standing in your way. Remember that you are where you are because of the decisions you have made, or failed to make. It is your responsibility to choose where you are going from one position in life to the next.

LEARN FROM MISTAKES

My wife and I have made plenty of mistakes in our marriage and with our children during the early stages of our relationship. When our children didn't live up to our expectations we demanded that they improve and follow our instructions. In addition to our demands for doing things right or correcting a deficiency, we criticized them. Our older children bore the consequences of our ignorance. We actually thought that we were right, that criticism would correct them, and they would eventually comply. It was just the opposite! Our children rebelled and resented us. Thank God they never got to the point where they wanted to seek revenge. You must realize that parents make costly mistakes because they may lack the knowledge and skills to use positive suggestions and instructions all of the time.

During one of our recent family meetings, my wife and I apologized to our children for our own ignorance, and we asked for their forgiveness.It was extremely important to us that they know we did not mean to hurt them and that we regreted the negative consequences they may have experienced. Never criticize your parents or anyone else. It does not help them or the situation.

GIVE MORE. GET MORE

Haven't you heard all of your life that *" to give is better than to receive."* This is absolutely true. If you give more, according to the law of sowing and reaping, you will get more. If you give less you will receive less. And yes, if you give nothing, you will absolutely get nothing.

My youngest daughters and I have a game we play. I will say, "If you give more..." They will respond by saying, "You'll get more." On the other hand, they know, automatically, the opposite response, without my even suggesting it." You give a little, you'll get a little." When you manage your parents by giving more in a positive, proactive and productive way, the benefits and the rewards you receive are plentiful!

PERMISSION

Always ask for permission in advance. My daughter had a habit of asking for permission to go to a friend's house to spend the night just as the friend was on the way to pick her up. This placed my wife and I in an uncomfortable position because we do not like to make hasty decisions. Why risk an unfavorable outcome by rushing us for permission? Sometimes, we would flat-out tell her "no!" Saying "no" to her caused us to be unhappy, because we had to deny her requests and she was not happy with our unfavorable responses. In our case, we were not responsible for placing ourselves in the position of having to make hasty decisions. However, our daughter probably felt we were responsible for the negative outcomes each time. If she had known how to manage us and had kept us informed ahead of time, we would have granted more of her requests.

HOLD YOUR TONGUE

If your mom and dad raise an objection, begin managing this situation by listening to understand their point of view. This may require you to hold your tongue. Their opinion is the real issue, as they see it. Until you convince them otherwise, they will not be willing to see things your way. Nodding your head to let them know you are aware of their objection gives them a sense that you understand their feelings.

Emphatic agreement is the first crucial step to disarming and minimizing resistance and objections. This barrier will not go away unless your parents believe that you understand their position. The moment you get in tuned to your parents' feelings, they will be more likely to listen to you. This is a good opportunity for negotiating and explaining the benefits they will receive by giving their approval. When your parents realize the value of what you are saying, they will be motivated to give you the permission you are seeking.

Why wouldn't your parents give you permission? Here are some reasons:

- *They do not trust you.*

- *You did not live up to some past agreement or expectation.*

- *They do not believe what you tell them.*

- *They do not see the need.*

The *condition of uncertainty* must be removed, simply because parents will give their permission only if they trust you. They will not say you are not telling the truth, but they will wonder how can they be sure you are going to do what you say. You have already made a decision to change for the better. Now, you must speak the truth regardless of the circumstances. Be honest, trustworthy, dependable, and reliable.

LET THEM SEE THE NEED

There is no point of trying to get your parents' permission to go somewhere or do something that is unsafe. How can you avoid this? Simple. Do those things which are safe and rewarding. Think ahead of time. If you get an idea about something in particular, test your own thinking. Ask other reliable adults what they think about your idea. If you receive feedback that is unfavorable, this is a clear indication that "it won't fly" with your parents.

The best way to get your parents to see value in what you want to do is to think objectively. Make the best decision and then seek their approval.

THE "PARENT ADVOCATE"

If your parents grant your brothers or sisters permission to do something, they have a reason for making a favorable decision. If you have made the same request and were denied, do not criticize their decision or compare their response to the one they gave your siblings. This is the time to ask your brother or sister how they got permission. Be your own *"Parent advocate."*

Another reason parents will not give you permission is because they are feeling pressured or rushed. Give them a chance to think things over. They may like what you are requesting, but do not want to make any definite decisions at the time. Sometimes, your parents just want to forget about your request, unless you have taken the appropriate actions to remove the *haste barrier.* If mom and dad really want to think things over before giving their permission, it is because they are afraid of making a decision that they might regret later on. Your strategy is to reduce the risk of them saying "no," and increase their desire to say "yes". When you reduce their fears by increasing their benefits, the *haste barrier* will disappear.

Remember there are no guarantees of success in this area. Their objections show that your parents are interested, but not convinced. In other words, they may be telling you they like your request, but they have to clear a few things up, first.

IT'S OKAY TO KEEP ASKING

If you make a request or seek your parents' permission to do something, they might say "no". Keep asking. Ask at least six times before you decide to give up on your request. Use the *"spaced asking"* technique. This works on everyone, especially adults. If you notice how young children approach their parents, you can learn something.

My eight and ten year old daughters get what they want from my wife and I, almost 100 percent of the time. Why are they successful? How are they successful? Because, young children do not take "no" personally when they are denied a request. My children can ask to go outside and play with the other children in the neighborhood. For whatever reason, we may tell them "no" they cannot go. They do not take our "no" reply personally. A few minutes later, they will come back and ask the same question. And of course, our reply will be, "didn't we just tell you no!" They will leave for a few more minutes ıly to come right back to ask for our permission, again.

With their persistence, our resistance starts to break down. They will make the same request in a timely fashion over and over again. I'll reply, "don't ask me, ask your mother." They will go to their mother and ask. And yes, my wife will send them right back to me. This back and forth process will continue; until finally to stop their persistence, in a raised voice I'll say "Go on, get out of here, and be careful!" See how they were successful in getting us to say "yes" to their request. Why? Because, they did not take our refusal personally and they persisted until they got their way. Our children simply melted down our resistance.

You too, can be just as successful as younger children with the win-win outcome. That is, of course, if you remember to use the spaced asking technique by not taking a "no" personally and using good negotiating techniques. If you are refused a request because of your parent's objection, reassess your request and ask again. Tactful persistence is the key to success.

If you do not believe what I have just said, take this into account. Of the salespeople who ask for orders:

- *44 percent give up after the first "no."*

- *22 percent give up after the second "no."*

- *14 percent give up after the third "no."*

- *12 percent give up after the fourth "no."*

These numbers total up to 92 percent. However, most salespeople never ask the fifth time around.

The salespeople who do ask for the fifth and sixth time make about 80 percent of all sales. You should also know that 60 percent of all their customers say "no" the first four times before they finally say "yes." This is definitely consistent with Biblical scriptures, **"Seek and ye shall find. Ask, and it shall be given unto you."** Just keep asking. Remember there is no harm in asking mom and dad. Parents can only give you one of two answers, yes or no. You have a 50 percent chance of success, initially. And, this percentage increases each time you ask for your parent's approval.

THE DARKEST HOUR IS JUST BEFORE DAWN

The next time you get discouraged because of your parents' refusal, remember *"the darkest hour is just before dawn"* and something wonderful is about to happen. *"Surely after difficulty comes ease. Surely after difficulty comes ease. But when thy immediate task has been removed, still strive harder."* Like many other skills practice increases your chances of success. How can your successes be measured? By the number of approvals and the number of times you are recognized for a quality relationship.

MOTIVATING YOUR PARENTS

One of the greatest gratifications you will experience is your parents becoming involved with you positively. To accomplish and achieve goals with your parents will require motivation.

MOTIVATION IS AN INTERNAL PROCESS

Getting your parents involved is going to be a wonderful experience. This type of positive gratification does not happen or develop by chance. What you will come to realize is that your parents have become motivated to assist you in managing them. How has this occurred? You hear a lot of talk on motivation. You are constantly told to be self-motivated or to be a motivated human being. In order to motivate your parents towards peak participation, you must understand motivation.

WHAT IS MOTIVATION?

Look at the word motivation. *Motivation* is a word that comes from the word "motive". Motive is defined as an internal drive that causes a person to act in a positive or negative way. People who are motivated will do things without being told to do them. They will be interested in what they are doing with an apparent undying determination to succeed. When a person is motivated regarding a particular project or activity, it is hard to discourage him or her. And, when a

78

person is uninterested and bored with a project or activity, it is very difficult to get him or her to participate. In learning how to set goals, you ask the question, "What's in it for me?" If you create an environment that allows your parents to become more interested in you, everyone in the family will benefit.

CREATE A POSITIVE ENVIRONMENT FOR MOTIVATION

How can you create an environment that motivates your parents? Be dependable, reliable, proactive, sincere, and committed to your parents. It will "turn them on", because there is something in it for all of you. They will become pleased when a positive environment exists around them.

Know that parents are motivated most when they are happy and like what they are doing. You cannot motivate other people. What you can do in managing your parents is to "create an environment" where motivation occurs naturally. You can help your parents "turn themselves on" so that they will be motivated to help you.

THE FEAR OF FAILURE

Why aren't people motivated? Usually it's a *fear of failure or a fear of rejection*. Understanding these two destructive attitudes will allow you to create an environment for change and positive growth.

You may anticipate your parents being somewhat hesitant, doubtful, or even a little curious after you express your intention to improve the relationship. Initially, your parents might be receptive when they realize your desire for a positive change. Because you are programmed in many ways to fail, doubt may set in later. Remember, their participation is essential for your successful efforts.

You are created to succeed, but programmed to fail. With your proactive efforts, you will reprogram yourself to succeed rather than to fail. From time to time, you may not succeed right away. *Know that it is okay to take calculated risks in order to succeed.*

PART 9

PERSONAL DEVELOPMENT

I often tell people that, *other than God, I like me more than I like anyone else. I care for me more than I care for anyone else.* If what I have stated sounds conceited, it is not and it is not meant to be taken that way. Please understand, in order to help others, you must ask for the assistance of God Almighty. You must ask your Creator to help you so that you can help others. If you want to improve the quality of others, you must improve the quality of yourself. If you want to improve the relationship with your parents, you must improve the relationship with yourself. Successful managers are life-long learners. Always be in a state of renewal and evolution. Improving yourself is not a selfish or conceited act. God asks you to be charitable. Give charity to others for their benefit, but, also to save your own soul. Give so you can receive, or be rewarded in the "hereafter" for your good deeds. There is a saying that *"charity begins at home and then it is spread abroad."* Help yourself, first, in order that you may be able to help others.

LIKE YOURSELF MORE THAN YOU LIKE ANYONE ELSE

I mentioned liking "me" more than I liked anyone else, other than God Almighty. The same applies to you. You should like "you" more than you like anyone else other than God Almighty. It is okay to feel this way. In order to help others, you must help yourself. In order to like others, you must like yourself. Sometimes, you forget about yourself. God provides you with 24 hours to work with each day. Some people believe this is not enough time. You may be so used to "being so busy" and doing other things for people, that you might be neglecting yourself. When was the last time you saw the sun set? How many good books have you read lately? Are you fit and in good shape? What about that exercise program? What about your health? Do you spend time with your family and the people who are important to you? Are you taking care of yourself like you should? It is vital you take care of yourself so that you can care for

80

others, especially when managing your parents.

The statement I make about liking "me" more than anyone else reminds me to take care of myself by remaining physically fit, emotionally stable, spiritually uplifted, and healthy. You must spend time by yourself, just for the sake of you. Personal development includes continuing education and training. You need a constant flow of education and training to improve your life. I highly recommend reading at least six nonfiction books of interest a year. Reading keeps the mind active, alert and sharp. Reading keeps your imagination alive, and your mind in a "ready to be used" mode. The average person finishing high school or college reads less than one book a year! Try reading more than one book a year. Reading at least six books a year will place you in the "top" five percent category of the people who read in America. Keep your personal development constant for a lifelong improvement.

YOUR CAR STEREO AS A SOURCE OF EDUCATION

Listen to uplifting and encouraging information that makes you feel positive. Listen to "personal development" seminars on audio tapes while driving. Listen to religious topics involving scriptures. This is a good time to learn how to reinforce information with very little effort. The average person spends up to 500 hours in their vehicle, each year. This equals two college semesters a year. Use the tape player in your car or a walkman cassette player as a personal development resource. Watch personal development video seminars. Attend personal development seminars, whenever possible. Leave anti-social, counterproductive, destructive movies, television programs and music alone! Keep your mind constantly fed with positive and constructive information. Feeding your mind with this kind of information will bring rewarding results.

AS A MAN THINKTH, SO IS HE

Remember, *you become what you think about.* The mind is like a huge sponge that absorbs all kinds of information. The subconscious takes in information without discrimination. It cannot distinguish "good from bad", "right from wrong", "truth from falsehood".

It just simply stores everything, including smells, sounds, feelings, and any other experiences. It is said that *"As a man thinkth... so is he."* The mind is a very powerful, sophisticated and complex tool.

Be sure you feed your mind and involve yourself in positive, productive and wholesome activities. The results of these activities and experiences will translate into positive, productive behavior.

Watch your self-talk. *Self-talk* is what you are constantly thinking, saying, or contemplating. Most self-talk is harmless. For instance, you may have thoughts about taking your car to a mechanic for repairs, making a doctor's appointment, going grocery shopping, the type of exercise you may want to engage in, and so on. Such examples of self-talk are:

"I hate going to that auto shop for repairs."

"Every time I drive on this street, I get a traffic ticket."

"I know I'm not going to find a parking space."

Some forms of negative self-talk that can have an impact on your mental or physical condition are phrases like:

"She makes me sick."

"I can't write well."

"I can't lose weight because..."

"I don't like to drive in rainy weather."

"I'm terrible when it comes to remembering peoples' names."

"I'm not good in math."

"Mondays are never good for me."

"I don't ever win anything."

Notice that when you are "self-talking", it is always in a personal sense and present tense. These conversations to yourself will program your subconscious. Your subconscious will take on these suggestions as commands. When self-talk is based upon what you believe, it can become your reality, positive or negative. This means it can work for you or against you. For example, if you believe that every time you take a final exam you are going to do poorly on the exam because of the pressure, these thoughts occur in your inner conversation when final exam time comes. This means you will probably fulfill your expectations of doing poorly on the exam. If you believe you are going to do well on the exam, the results are more likely to be positive, based upon the same principle. Self-talk has to be monitored so you can use it for your own benefit. Be careful and be positive when you talk to yourself.

ATTITUDE

You hear a great deal about attitude. You are told to have a good attitude; that a positive attitude will get you into places you want to be; that your attitude has a lot to do with how people perceive you. You hear people say, "He or she has a good or bad attitude;" that *it is your attitude and not your aptitude that counts most.*

According to the dictionary, *attitude* is a mental mood; a mental position or feeling about a subject, object or circumstance. Right away, you can see the correlation between attitude and self-esteem. How you think has a direct relationship to how you feel about yourself.

Now you recognize the importance of feeling good about yourself. Please understand, it is okay to like yourself and feel good about yourself. Use positive affirmations to help you. Repeat 20 to 50 times, "I like myself" three or four times a day. This simple, but powerful affirmation will raise the level of your self-esteem.

A GOOD ATTITUDE WORKS MIRACLES

Yes! A positive attitude can carry you a very long way in this life, and with others. Your attitude tells others what to expect from you almost instantly.

And guess what! You can control your attitude! You must remember, however, you are in control of you and no one else.

When people see you, they make judgments based on your attitude. Remember, you are constantly sending out messages about yourself, verbally and nonverbally. You are constantly sending signals to others about how you feel and think. Sometimes, you are not able to tell what is causing a person to think and feel the way he or she does. But, you can recognize that person's mood from facial expressions, body posture, and attitude. You can see the way they carry themselves, what they say, and most importantly, what that person does.

ACTIONS SPEAK LOUDER THAN WORDS

What you do tells exactly what you believe. What's going on inside you, will manifest itself through your actions! A good attitude, or even better, a great attitude equals great results. Attitude is reflected in your actions, which produce results, which is reflected by progress, which is reflected in how successful you are.

PEOPLE WILL KNOW

People may know instantly if they are going to be confronted with a good experience or a bad experience by your attitude. You can tell when people are going to have a good or a bad day. You can look at people and tell if they are not feeling well, if they are sad, if they are happy, if they are in good health, or if they feel good about themselves. You should have an attitude of gratitude. Your attitude should be that of a successful human being who is making a positive contribution to life. If you have a great attitude towards the relationship with your parents, they will too.

SPEND TIME WITH YOURSELF

Another great technique that will benefit you greatly is spending time by yourself. Spend at least one hour a day in solitude.

Get in a quiet, empty place where there aren't any interruptions. A nice park or beach, the mountains or the lake - anyplace where you can hear the sounds of nature are perfect settings for solitude. If you are unable to escape to places like these, a quiet room you can have all to yourself and not be disturbed is a great place. Just sit or lay down and be completely still and relaxed. Allow your mind to free itself! Let your mind wander in any direction it wants to go. You may close your eyes or keep them open. Get in a relaxed position and allow your thoughts to float for at least 30 minutes to an hour. This form of exercise will help your mind to realign itself. Spending time by yourself, with yourself, is definitely a positive form of personal development. Use this exercise and practice other relaxation techniques so you can become a renewed individual.

GREAT PEOPLE MEDITATE

Most "great" people throughout history, including prophets and messengers, spent much time in meditation. There are several books about meditation which can teach you this valuable practice. I urge you to familiarize yourself with the art of meditation, especially the use of relaxation and visualization.

PHYSICAL EXERCISE IS VERY IMPORTANT

Physical exercise is definitely a part of personal development. I cannot stress enough the importance of getting into good physical condition and staying that way. It is recommended that you get at least 30 minutes of exercise three times a week for a good, stable cardiovascular condition. Being healthy enhances every aspect of managing your parents. Good health and physical fitness have a direct impact on your energy level, your mental attitude, and spiritual aspirations.

Watch what you put into that "magnificent" body of yours. Remember, *you are what you eat.* So, learn how to "eat to live." It is written, *"eat of the good things which God has provided for you, but do not overindulge."*

Read books on nutrition, how the body's energy system works, the body's peak performance, exercise physiology, and the relationship between good eating habits and good physical conditioning. Being physically fit allows you to achieve your goals a lot faster.

85

DRUGS

You can't discuss personal development without considering the issue of drugs. It is very important that you understand the reasons why you should always remain sober relative to managing your parents. There are tons of scientific evidence which have accumulated over the past 50 years regarding the use of drugs, drug abuse, and the damage that can be caused by abusing drugs. Studies have concluded that marijuana, cocaine, heroin, LSD, and other drugs can cause massive damage to the brain's cellular process, the reproductive system, the circulatory system, and the respiratory system. The principal ingredients in most of these drugs tend to accumulate in the brain and, as a result, create a serious possibility of brain damage, physical aggression, distorted perception of reality, chronic passivity, and lack of motivation. I believe that any drug taken for a purpose other than legal medical reasons is harmful, especially when it is abused.

AVOID THE TEMPTATION

You may be invited by your friends or acquaintances to try an illegal drug. Be firm in your resolve to remain sober and drug-free. It is said that the adolescent years, between the ages of 14 and 20, are the most challenging time of life. Seeking knowledge and understanding this period in your life will prepare you for pressured situations. According to research, one out of two people in America drinks or has tried some kind of illegal drug. It appears that drug abuse in this country is indiscriminate. Making decisions to manage your parents requires you to make sound and rational choices. Avoid any use of illegal drugs or abuse of controlled substances, and remain "clear headed."

PART 10

GOAL SETTING AND TIME MANAGEMENT

The next part of the plan is to set goals for what you want to accomplish in a timely manner. Days can be spent discussing goal setting and time management because of the importance these two things play in the success of high achieving people.

HOW TO SET THEM, HOW TO ACHIEVE THEM

The lack of training in "goal setting" as well as how to achieve goals is a real problem in society. Throughout your life, in high school and in college, there probably hasn't been a requirement or course to teach you how to set goals. Everywhere you go you hear people telling you that you must have goals. Children, while growing up, and adults on the job are told by their parents and supervisors to set and achieve goals. But no one ever teaches you how to develop goals or how to achieve them. If you follow these instructions when setting goals, you will become one of three percent of the population that has this skill.

BE ONE OF THE 3 PERCENT, AND WIN!

A study was conducted at Harvard University in 1952 to determine if students set goals and actually wrote them down on paper. Only 3 percent of the students honestly knew how to set and achieve goals. During the next 20 years, these same students were tracked in reference to their successes. In 1972, the three percent who set goals were earning more in terms of money than the other 97 percent combined.

In fact less than 5 percent of the US population makes over $100,000 per year. According to other reports, only 2 percent of the population controls the nation's wealth. Why is this important to know? If you study successful people, especially self-made millionaires, you will find that they all have one thing in common. They are "goal setters". Goals are absolutely critical if you are going to be successful, not only in managing your parents, but for your life in general. Great emphasis should be placed on goal setting, and most importantly, on how to achieve them.

WHY PEOPLE DO NOT SET GOALS

With so much emphasis placed on goal setting, you may wonder why so few people set goals. If this is such an important skill, why is it that only a few people know how to set goals. The main reason most people do not set goals is because they have never been taught how. Another reason why people do not set goals is because they have no desire. They have not been motivated to do anything in a particular area, and as a result, goal setting just doesn't interest them.

WHAT ARE GOALS?

What are goals? How do we set goals? How do we achieve them? A *goal* is a specific desire, with a date of completion, to accomplish what you want to do. A true goal fits the "SMART" formula. It must be:

> **S**PECIFIC
> **M**EASURABLE
> **A**TTAINABLE
> **R**EALISTIC
> **T**IMELY

STEP ONE - VISUALIZE AND DREAM

The first step in goal setting is to make the goal "SMART". The goal has to be *specific,* not a generality. It must distinctly and plainly set forth a definite desire. It must be explicit. In setting goals, you must identify, specifically, what it is you want to do. How can you identify what you want to do? Brainstorm. Think about what you want to do. Dream about what you want or want to do.

Visualize being successful and reaching your goals. The importance of visualization cannot be over-emphasized. When you visualize or see yourself accomplishing your goals, this provides future direction for you. A vision guides you daily in a rapidly changing time. It is important that you share that goal or vision with your parents. Shared visions create shared values within the relationship. Vision provides the driving force within the relationship.

You will need to have a vision in order to attract and build a relationship, instill commitment, and develop alliance. Create a "wish list" of places you would like to see, things you would like to be, do, and have in your life.

Visualize your education, career, business, and how much money you would like to make. Visualize the size of your family, the kind of person you want to marry, and how you want to get along with people. Visualize your spiritual development, your health, and how you want to live. It is said that "where there is no vision, the people perished."

PLACE THEM ON PAPER

Once you have developed a list of goals you would like to pursue, write them down. Your goals have to be in quantities, weights, heights, amounts, distances, numbers, etc. For example, if you want to lose or gain weight, identify how much you would want to weigh. Your goal would be the pounds you actually desire to loose, gain or weight. Another example is having a desire to be rich. How rich do you want to be? Identify how much money or how many assets it would take for you to be rich. This is the process of getting to the specifics in goal setting.

VERIFY YOUR GOAL EFFORTS

The goal has to be ***measurable.*** You must be able to verify what you achieve or set out to do. For instance, if your goal is to bench-press 100 pounds, the measuring criteria would be the number of pounds you bench pressed (50 pounds, 70 pounds, 95 pounds, etc.) If you wanted to lose 15 pounds, the verification would be the number of pounds you actually lost. If you wanted to run the 100-meter race in ten seconds, the measurement would be the number of seconds you actually ran that distance. Goals must have some kind of standard of comparison. You will determine or make your adjustments by a form of verification, standard, or measurement.

IS IT ATTAINABLE?

The goal has to be *attainable.* Your goal has to be something that you can attain and not something that is impossible. You must be able to say that in time with the exertion of your body and mind, you will be able to reach your goal.

IS IT REAL?

The goal has to be *realistic.* Your goal has to be something that is real or reasonable, and not something that is impossible or unreasonable. You would not set a goal that you knew could cause injury or damage to yourself and others. The goal has to be morally fair. The goal has to be lawful.

IS IT TIMELY?

The goal has to be *timely.* Doing things on time is extremely important. Be time conscious. It is important to know if it is time for you to set a goal in a certain area or not. Timing is everything. What is a timely goal? A timely goal is when all of your decisions are in accord with each other; having the right idea at the right time to meet certain needs. Think of timing as though you were shooting at a target with a bow and arrow. You could place the bow in your hand and point the arrow towards the target. However, as you point the arrow in an attempt to hit the bulls-eye, your hands and eyes have to be coordinated and the release of the arrow from the bow has to coordinate with the hands and the eyes. So is it with your goals. Have the right idea at the right time for certain needs or desires. Developing a plan of action will insure your goals will be achieved on time. Make sure you set your goals on time and know when each goal's time has come. Look for opportunities to set goals based on past, current, and projected conditions.

STEP TWO

Identify the specific date you want to have your goal completed. There must be a time limit for achieving that goal. The time limit or date will drive you towards your goal. Being conscious of the completion date simply generates additional motivation that you will need in accomplishing your goal.

STEP THREE

Identify the obstacles and challenges you will have to overcome in order to achieve your goals. Prepare yourself for the challenges you are going to face. An obstacle may be self-doubt or laziness. You will be able to conquer these when you follow the remaining steps.

STEP FOUR

Identify the people, organizations, and resources that can help you to achieve your goals. Make as many friends as possible! Having people that can assist you in achieving your goals can save you a lot of time and money. Align yourself with powerful people. "Fly with the eagles and leave the turkeys alone." Avoid those people who do not support your achievement. Think of the organizations that can assist you, and the resources they may have. Organizations can be in the form of churches, community groups, state and local agencies, businesses, or magazines and newspapers.

STEP FIVE

Identify the knowledge, training, education, and skills you are going to need to achieve your goal. This is a very important step. You must spend the necessary time training and educating yourself.

STEP SIX

Step six, is to write out a clear, step-by-step plan of action. A ***plan of action*** is a blue-print. It serves as a guide for your goals. It is a systematic approach, and a number of instructions that will get you from point A to point B to point C, and so on. Most people never plan out what they want to do. For instance, most people spend lots of time planning their weddings, but spend little or no time planning their marriages. Think about your plan of action relative to managing your parents.

The plan of action must be written in a positive, first person, present tense. For example, if your goal is to earn $100,000 a year, your plan of action may start out like this. *"I am currently working as a supervisor in my company.*

I am meeting with my supervisor to discuss and identify ways to increase my salary. I am conducting an ongoing assessment of my earnings and worth. I am performing my immediate job assignment with excellence to justify to my supervisor a pay increase.

I am asking for additional hours to work overtime so I can earn additional money. I am working part-time jobs for other companies or organizations to earn extra money. I am saving 90 percent of all money earned as a result of overtime or extra jobs. I am making myself more valuable to my supervisors in order to command their attention for my pay increase."

This is just one example of a plan of action. Your plan of action to manage your parents should be complete and just as clear.

STEP SEVEN

Write down the question, "What's in it for me if I achieve my goal?" Then list the answers. Think of the most selfish ways reaching your goals will benefit you. These questions and answers will motivate you tremendously toward your goals. The answer to the question, "What's in it for me" also reminds you why you want to achieve your goals when you are faced with challenges.

STEP EIGHT

Review your goals at least once a day. It keeps you clear about what you want to do. Looking at your goals is like driving a car home. You must keep your eyes on the road at all times to make sure you don't run off, or hit someone or something.

Keeping your eyes on the road allows you to look at all the signs, in addition to the speed limit you need to observe during travel to your destination. Look at your goals as a drive home. Keep your eyes on your goals so that you will not end up in places you don't want to be. Review your goals every day. Keep them written in small phrases on index cards or a sheet of paper that can be easily looked at and put away.

Looking at your goals also programs them into your subconscious mind. As you continue to place your goals into your subconscious, your conscious will take these instructions as a command and bring them into reality.

Visualize your goals being accomplished in detail. See the "big picture." A picture is worth a thousand words.

Let yourself feel the sensations, the emotions, the happy feelings, and even the actual touching of the goals which are tangible. Feel the handshakes and hugs from those who will want to honor you for achieving your goals. Hear the responses from yourself and others when you achieve your goals. Hear the positive comments, the expressions of people's surprise, and the congratulations!

The more feeling, touching, seeing, smelling, or even tasting of your goals you visualize, the better. The feedback from your senses drives the goals into your subconscious so you will have an automatic system in place working for you. Your five senses provide instant and accurate feedback toward achieving your goals. Research shows that:

- *If you hear it, you'll forget it.*
- *If you see it, you'll remember it.*
- *If you do it, you'll understand it.*

The more senses involved in visualizing your goals, the more excited and motivated you become about reaching them.

STEP NINE

Rewrite your goals every 30 days. This allows you to make modifications in upgrading your goals. It reinforces what you want to do. It programs the subconscious and motivates you to achieve your goals. Now, identify two goals that you can work on everyday. *As soon as you accomplish a goal, immediately replace it with another.*

STEP TEN

Set a six-month goal, a twelve-month goal, a two-year goal, a five-year goal, and then a desired ten-year goal.

OBJECTIVES

Goals are different than objectives. *Objectives* are the reasons why, the purposes, the benefits, and the results of reaching your goals. Unlike goals, objectives can be general. You may have as many objectives as you want listed relative to your goals.

KEEP THEM SECRET

In addition to these ten basic steps, I want you to remember another important thing about setting your goals. Never, never share your personal goals with anyone.

If you share your goals with other people, they may not understand what it is you want to accomplish. Usually, because people do not understand you or your goals, they may try to discourage you with negative remarks. Someone, out of doubt and ignorance, may say that "you can't do it" because it is too "big" for you to achieve. And, as a result, you may change your mind about your own goals! Sometimes, people are jealous and will criticize or discourage you from reaching high goals. Protect yourself. Don't tell anyone about your goals, and keep pushing forward.

Use these steps in goal setting and see an increase in your success. Ask these questions. Is this my goal? Is my goal legal and moral? The answers to these questions must always be yes. Review your goals daily after you have written them on paper. Work on at least two of your goals every day. Develop and work on goals that will allow you to achieve other goals.

These ten steps will yield remarkable results for you. Remember desire, expectations, imagination, and the will to succeed are key factors in goal setting.

TIME MANAGEMENT

It is said, "time is of the essence" which means you should go about using your time wisely. You have 24 hours per day to work with, no more, no less. In order to achieve your goals and manage your parents, you have to learn to manage your time. How you use your time will determine if you are successful or unsuccessful. You must be on time and do things on time, or you will be out of touch with what is going on. Projects and activities you are involved in will not turn out the way you want them to if they are not on time.

USE YOUR TIME WISELY

Write down what and how you spend your time in brief phrases for a period of seven days. Once you have collected this information, examine it. Study what you are doing with your time. Look at the period of time when you are most productive. Eliminate or minimize periods of time when you are the least productive.

Use your time wisely, especially during transition and waiting periods. Transition time is a period when you travel in your vehicle, on an airplane, and in other forms of transportation. Usually, you are not on a planned vacation or some planned outing during this period. Waiting time is a period when you are waiting for some kind of service. Waiting in a doctor or dentist's office provides a great opportunity for utilization of time. You should be able to think of many more places or locations you can or may experience transitional or waiting time. These times are perfect for listening to personal development audio tapes, using a laptop computer, reading a book, or completing written assignments.

BE PREPARED

Always carry a note pad to jot down spontaneous "great" ideas which come to mind. Read good books, positive news articles, or constructive publications. Collect articles about self improvement and other topics of interest.

GET ORGANIZED

Get organized. Organize your briefcase, notebook, desk, room, closet and other areas for easy access or filing of material. When you become organized, this produces credibility for you in the eyes of your parents. Get control of your telephone procedures and habits. When you are not at home or work, have message pads available.

Voice-mail or answering service can be very effective, if you give clear instructions to the caller. The caller should be instructed to leave a detailed message and a return number. This allows you to work on the person's concern before you contact or call them back. Pagers can also be very helpful in managing your time and schedule.

Minimize talking on the telephone. At times, you may have to talk to people regarding legitimate concerns. However, if talking on the telephone becomes frequent and/or lengthy, your parents' perception may be that you are "wasting" time. Avoid this perception by visiting or writing letters to your party.

TIME FOR YOU

Although you may have the makings of a "happy life" for yourself, you can find yourself growing apart from your parents because of the lack of time. With your own families, schools, careers, and other personal responsibilities, you may find yourself having no time for yourself. Time for yourself and your loved ones is precious. With your personal life, family and career, a lot of creativity is needed to avoid self-neglect. Managing, after all, requires time.

USE GOOD JUDGMENT

Depriving yourself of personal time can take its toll. You may feel overwhelmed by the demands that managing your parents entails. If you add a job, personal life, school, financial concerns, and other challenges to the list, the amount of time you have left for yourself shrinks even more. Giving to your parents can sometimes lead to frustration. You may blame them for your feeling overloaded. Reassess your time management, say "no" to the nonessentials and make a proper decision to get the best results.

If you are an adult, your role as your parent's child has evolved.

You have the same responsibilities of maintaining your own lives and earning a family living. Some parents and children grow apart due to these conditions and responsibilities while others grow closer. You can maintain your closeness by constantly monitoring what you are doing on a day to day basis. To maintain closeness, consider which of those responsibilities are essential and necessary, and which ones have some flexibility. You may need to adjust your schedule and plans to meet the needs of your own private and professional life. Plan each day with a written daily planner. If you fail to plan, you are actually planning to fail. Plan your work and work your plan with a good time management system.

PART 11

BECOME A FAVORITE CHILD

When you begin managing your parents, some of your relatives may become a little jealous. I caution you to be aware of this. *You are going to receive a lot of attention for your positive efforts. One thing is certain; you would rather have them a little jealous of you than to have the displeasure of mom and dad. Besides, who is more important?*

My brothers, sisters, and other relatives recognized that I was different and unique as a child. My curiosity, willingness to learn, and the deep love and affection I had for my family, especially my mother, were very noticeable. I was often teased by my relatives for asking lots of questions about various things. I knew at a very early age that we were poor. We did not have the kind of lifestyle or the resources we saw in other neighborhoods, on television or in books and magazines. There were many of us in the small houses we lived in growing up in Atlanta. Often, because they were poor too, some of my aunts, uncles and cousins lived with us.

LET THEM SEE THE GOOD SIDE OF YOU

Regardless of our financial situation, I was determined not to disappoint my mother. I never allowed her to see me in a negative light. Nor did I embarrass her or do anything she would be ashamed of. Now, don't think I was an angel. I was not, but it was important to me that my mother thought I was. I was a normal child when it came to experiencing and experimenting with the typical things youngsters do while growing up. Occasionally, I got into trouble. I got into fights. And I made bad grades and skipped school sometimes.

What made me unusual was my ability to be focused and serious when it was time to. I disciplined myself to do the things I should do, whether I liked doing those things or not. That made me different from my relatives. I wanted to please my mother and I wanted to be her favorite child. I was not the oldest or the youngest child, but I wanted to be number one because I had a self-serving interest!

I wanted to be able to gain my mother's favor and approval to do the things I wanted to do. I wanted her to be proud of me and as I grew into my teens, I recognized that I had become her "favorite" child.

BE A SPECIAL PERSON TO YOUR PARENTS

How did I become so favored? I knew my mother loved my brothers and sisters as well. She provided for all of us equally. But my relationship with my mother was absolutely special, and remains special to this today. Everyone knew it. We were special to each other. I would do everything I could to protect her, and she would do the same for me. I can remember asking her questions that some parents would have thought were strange, or even embarrassing. I felt that I could share anything with my mother. And often, I did share my thoughts with her. My mother never acted embarrassed or offended when I asked questions that were unusual or uncomfortable, and she was very careful not to hurt my feelings or discourage me from being curious or inquisitive.

WORK AT BECOMING A FAVORITE CHILD

I worked at becoming the favorite child. It did not just happen by chance. I wanted my mother's attention, love, affection and time. I developed a more proactive attitude as I recognized the attention I was receiving. I did the things that made my parents happy. I did what was expected of me. I went beyond what was expected of me by doing additional things that were positive and satisfying to my parents without being told to do them.

When I demonstrated proactive behavior, my parents' hope and trust in me increased even more. Good managers know to *"let people catch you doing something right."* I did just that. I often allowed them the opportunity to see me doing the right things without being told.

GET ALONG WITH
YOUR BROTHERS AND SISTERS

I did not treat my brothers and sisters unfairly or unjustly because I was the "favorite" child. On the contrary, I was helpful when I could be and supported them whenever I could.

THE LIST OF 100 THINGS

Make a list of 100 things that will make both mom and dad happy. You will call this list *"Mom and Dad's Happy List."* In addition to developing your list, sit with your parents and ask them to give you some areas they would like to see you do well in, or a list of things that would make them happy concerning you. (i.e., better grades in school, a clean and neat room, cutting the grass, washing the dishes, going to worship services, joining a school or civic committee or group, etc.).

As you develop your list, be creative until you have written down 100 things that would make mom and dad happy. Take as long as you need to develop your list. Add to your list each time you think of something new. Keep your list in a place where you can review it at least once a day. But, remember to start your list immediately! This is your private list which should not be shared with others. The more you do some of the things on your list, the more recognition and cooperation you will get from your parents. Expect to be treated better by your parents almost immediately!

STRENGTH SHOULD OUTWEIGH WEAKNESS

Hard work, enthusiasm, and dedication inspire others and flatter your parents. Put in extra effort in order to make things right with your parents. First impressions are lasting impressions. Get up early and straighten your room, and other places in your parent's home if you live with them. Use a daily planner. Planning will set the mood for you until the end of the day. After all, you are trying to impress them!

KEEP YOUR COMMITMENTS

Parents accept your shortcomings, as long as your strengths outweigh your weaknesses. What your parents cannot adjust to is uncertainty. If you say you are going to do something for them, keep your commitment.

If you say that you will do something, but fail to do it, your parents will doubt your dependability. If you realize that you cannot fulfill a commitment, let them know. Their disappointment will be far less than if they were to learn of it later on. It is better to be known for making an honest mistake than for being irresponsible.

FAMILY MEETINGS

Most families have unwritten rules which govern the way they function. Suggest having a 30 to 60 minute family meeting at least once a week. This will allow for those unwritten rules to be understood and expectations to be clarified. You should suggest or set up the meetings in accordance with your parents' time. Plan ahead, by communicating with your brothers and sisters regarding their participation. Prepare a written agenda for a smooth start, discussion, and finish. Your ability to organize will impress your parents.

Take care of all special events. Remember family birthdays and give heartwarming gifts. Often, gifts which are made by you which are genuine and original, are appreciated by your parents more than store bought ones. Sometimes, surprises are not a good idea. Occasionally, asking your parents what they need or would like for that special occasion is most appropriate and appreciated. Remember, if they give you their "wish list", let them know if you are unable to deliver on their requests or wishes.

If you ask your parents what they want for that special occasion, don't be surprised if they respond by saying, "I'll take whatever you give me." This kind of response may let you know that they might have everything they need. If you take the time to make a gift, even when they say they have everything they need, your parents will be truly touched. This will result in more good feelings within the relationship.

Look for unmet wants and needs. Ask your parents if there's anything else you can do? If they cannot identify anything, you may want to be proactive and suggest maybe taking them to a movie, shopping, or driving them to the park. Your mom and dad can't help but be very impressed by your efforts to exceed their expectations.

FIND WAYS TO BE HELPFUL

- *Take on unwanted chores or tasks. Learn a skill that's vital to your parents, or be the best at something no one else wants to do.*

- *Go the extra mile. Do what your parents expect of you and give a little extra. If you know the quality standards of certain jobs, complete those jobs and contribute a little more by being a "cut above the rest." Volunteer to help on a family matter that seems outstanding. Help out when there is an urgency at hand. Help your brothers and sisters complete their assignments. Compete with your brothers and sisters in doing good deeds.*

- *Work harder without being told to do so. For instance, you know how it is when mom and dad are away. Chores around the house just don't get done. Family members take their time. They lounge around, prepare snacks, and have friends come over to hang out. The upkeep of the house is neglected and soon the house is untidy and messy. Also, when parents are away, other family members have a tendency to bend the rules. The curfew time is stretched, talking on the telephone is excessive, and more disagreements with other family members occur. You should be aware of these conditions and do just the opposite. There is nothing mom and dad would appreciate more than to have a son or daughter handle situations in the appropriate manner when they are gone. The message you convey with this kind of approach will be long-lasting.*

- *Take credit for the whole family when appropriate. Allow other family members to share in the credit for something you did. They will have a tendency to help you in the near future.*

102

- *Develop a better relationship with your brothers and sisters. This creates harmony within the family and sets the tone for a constructive atmosphere.*

- *Become a mentor. No matter how old or young you are, help others by setting a good example. You can do this informally. You can also be a "big brother" or "sister" for your relatives. Mom and dad need as much assistance as possible keeping other family members in line. When you are such an example, they will not have to make any comparisons between you and other family members.*

WATCH WHAT YOU DO

Watch what you do because actions speak louder than words. Actions include your conduct, your etiquette, and your mannerisms. The Bible says, *"Judge a man by his deeds."* If you want to find out how a person thinks or what he or she believes, examine what that person does. Seeing is believing! Always be on your best conduct and exemplify good manners. You never know who's watching you or if that someone can either help or hurt you. Be on your best behavior, especially when mom and dad are around.

BE EXTRA POLITE

Always be extra polite and courteous to everyone. Run interference when interacting with your parents. Do things that make their lives easier. For example, observe the actions of waiters in restaurants. They are constantly seeking to please you during your visit at the eating establishment. If you get good service, you will want to leave a generous tip to show your appreciation. And like most people, the better the service, the greater the tip. Waiters realize it is their job to please you by providing prompt service and being polite. They are well aware that the better their service, the better their chances of being well rewarded. Like the waiter in the restaurant, remember that being extra polite and courteous to your parents will yield favorable rewards.

YES SIR - MA'AM

In addition to addressing your parents and other adults with "yes sir" or "no sir," "yes ma'am" or "no ma'am," you should address people as Mr., Miss or Mrs. when appropriate.

This way of addressing your parents and others will place you "a cut above the rest" when people think of you or when your name is mentioned.

If your parents comment in a negative way about you or a particular situation, respond by saying, "yes ma'am" or "yes sir." These polite and submissive words, represent a major step in avoiding conflict. The technique of being polite, humble, and apologetic disarms your parents who are angry or upset. After listening and acknowledging your parents with yes ma'am or sir, prepare to turn the situation around. Ask what can you do to correct or improve it. They will respond by recommending a task you can accomplish. Be willing to follow their recommendation, again, unless it is something unlawful, immoral or unethical. The more you use this kind of attitude, the easier it will become to manage your parents.

AVOID JOKING

Never play jokes on your parents. Jokes can go wrong more often than they can go right. Never allow anyone else to coax you into playing jokes on your parents. Because of the serious risks you might take by joking or playing pranks on your parents, you stand to lose more by making them very annoyed or angry with you. Leave the joking to the comedians.

REPORTING YOUR WHEREABOUTS

If you live with your parents, keep them informed of your whereabouts when leaving the house. Always let them know when you are leaving, where you are going, and when you are expected to return. Leaving their house without telling them where you are going and when you are returning is a sign of disrespect. Keeping them informed regarding your whereabouts gives them a sense of trust about you. As parents, your mom and dad will always feel that your whereabouts is their business. Your parents do not want control over you in the sense of a servant/master relationship but they do feel responsible for you. You will always be their child. Therefore, keep them informed.

BE ON THE LOOKOUT

If you arrive home before your parents get there, be ready to welcome them home and assist with carrying packages and parcels. Make them feel welcome by meeting them at the car and opening doors for them (mom's first). Parents love that and it makes everyone feel good.

BE A PROBLEM SOLVER

No one likes to be told to do things they don't like. In order to get your parents to accept your ideas, deal only in solutions rather than problems. Offer solutions versus problems to your parents. Your parents will be more receptive to your solutions. ***Provide answers to your parents in order to avoid them telling you what to do.*** Take the burden off your parents by giving solutions instead of problems.

When you offer solutions, they will respond by rewarding or complementing you. Search for answers before you are told to do so.

Here is a story that will help you understand the importance of being a problem-solver. *One day, our vehicle was in the shop for repairs. With eight children living at home, imagine the potential challenges we were going to face each day with a vehicle down. We had to get them to school and back, take them to swimming practice, and get ourselves to and from work. Elisha, our second oldest son, recognized our situation, took his younger siblings to and from school in his vehicle, and then to swimming practice. Late that evening, I called the natatorium to speak to the swim coach. I told the coach that I was on my way to pick up my children. The coach said, "Elisha is already here and getting ready to leave with them."* His mother and I greatly appreciate the things he did for us on that, and many other occasions. He made major contributions to the success of the family. He eased our burdens. Elisha was able to contribute, because he found solutions without being asked or told to do so. We said "thank you" in the presence of other family members and rewarded

105

him by offering to pay his car insurance for six months. These kinds of proactive, "solution finding" efforts will bring you recognition, appreciation and cooperation. Remember to do good deeds without thought to receiving anything in return.

The law of sowing and reaping will automatically take care of you. If you want positive things to happen for you, do good deeds for others, especially your parents.

BE RELIABLE.

More than anything else, your parents want to be able to depend on you. Specifically, this means:

·   *Do what you are supposed to do.*

·   *Do it when you say you are going to do it.*

·   *Do it right.*

·   *Complete it on time.*

Research shows that it takes twice the number of good deeds to wipe out the memory of a bad deed. This makes being reliable a top priority.

BE CREDIBLE

One thing parents need is peace of mind. And, who doesn't? Parents want to help you when you have their best interest at heart. Parents want security, integrity and assurance in the relationship. If you share information with your parents and keep it confidential as expected, you can become a credible person with them. If you say one thing and do another, this takes away from your credibility. Parents do not like hidden agendas.

FLY WITH THE EAGLES

If you associate with people of questionable character, your parents will begin to question your character. It is said, *"association with the people you are with most, brings assimilation.* " If you identify and associate with non-progressive people, you will become a non-progressive person. If you identify and be with progressive people, you will become a progressive person. Association does bring assimilation. So, interact with people who have positive qualities and a good direction in their lives.

BE RESPONSIVE

Being responsive simply means being available or accessible, and helping with challenges or problems. Keep your parents informed. Provide assistance as soon as possible. If your parents mention that their car needs servicing before they are to go on vacation, offer to take their car to a service station. The maintenance will be performed by the mechanics, and you will have provided a service for them. As a result, you can expect for them to be very grateful for your responsiveness.

BE EMPATHIC

Empathy means putting yourself in your parents' shoes and feeling what they feel. Visualize their condition by feeling or experiencing what they feel or experience. Listen, ask questions, express concern, and communicate on their level. Being empathetic will allow you to understand your parents. Recognize strengths and weaknesses so they may be used to compliment each other. Help your parents understand you. Treat each parent special.

BE PREPARED TO DO

On many occasions, you may think of your parents as people who give orders. Your parents brought you into this world as their children, and they expect instant and total obedience from you. If they tell you to do something, do it. When your parents act in this autocratic manner, *don't take it personally.* Be patient, stay in control, and think. For example, if you are told to make better grades in school, to clean up your room, wash the car, cut the grass, fix dinner or whatever it may be, be prepared to do it. Respond by saying "yes sir or ma'am" and complete what they have requested of you in an excellent manner. Wait for the opportunity to tell them you have completed what they asked of you, and ask if you can assist them in any other way.

When you have completed their requests with excellence, go to them and express your appreciation. You can say:

"Mom, dad, that was a good idea to wash the car at the time we did. It appears that it's not going to rain for a few days."

"When you let me fix dinner today, it gave me a chance to become a better cook. By the way, what's your favorite dish? Maybe I can make it for you next week."

"I'm glad we cut the grass today. The city crew came by and removed all the leaves and trash. The lawn really looks good now."

"Because you urged me to study like I did last semester, I made much better grades. Take a look at my report card."

INTRODUCE YOUR FRIENDS TO YOUR PARENTS

It is important for your parents to know that you socialize with positive and progressive people. Always introduce your parents to your closest friends. Whenever you are involved with someone like a boyfriend, girlfriend, fiance, a person you're dating, etc., introduce that person to your parents. This reduces the likelihood of your parents being suspicious about who you interact with. In addition, let your parents know in advance if you are bringing a guest to their house.

Your parents need to have privacy within their homes. Their homes should be protected and respected. If your friends are visiting you, make sure they are not roaming through your parents' house. Keep your friends from going into their private rooms or personal belongings without permission. Be responsible for your guest or guests by having them take a seat until you escort them to another part of the house. In order to avoid misunderstanding or embarrassment, let them know to dress modestly if they are spending the night.

BE EASY TO GET ALONG WITH

The Biblical scriptures say *"Be kind to one another, tender - hearted, forgiving one another."* Are you easy to get along with? Are you friends with your loved ones? If you can answer yes to these questions, then you probably don't commit the following acts:

· Criticizing others instead of praising them.

· Making insensitive comments.

· Neglecting others and their concerns.

· Creating a mockery, belittling, using insulting jokes towards others.

· Not listening.

· Being rude and inconsiderate.

Avoid these negative approaches. These actions will only devastate a relationship and prohibit forgiveness and healing of past hurts and pains. Treat your parents, brothers, sisters and other people with kindness and respect. Parents love this kind of treatment from their children! Pay special attention to those events when your parents are praising or recognizing your brothers or sisters for their good deeds. It's okay for mom and dad to see the good in each one of you. Encourage your brothers and sisters to do more good deeds so they will receive positive recognition.

Understand that each child means different things to each parent. They love you all, but sometimes there can be a "favorite" or "favorites." You can become a favorite by obeying them, doing good deeds, and exceeding expectations with excellence.

MAKE YOUR PARENTS LOOK GOOD!

Pay attention to the interactions which occur between relatives (aunts, uncles, cousins) and other friends of your parents. Establish and maintain a good relationship with them. Know their interests, such as their favorite subject, sport or team, topics of conversation, and likes or dislikes. The more you know about them, the more you can understand and appreciate their position within the family. Your parents, more than likely, value these individuals. Bring everyone closer for the benefit of your parents. Always make your parents "look good" in the eyes of others.

BORROWING MONEY

If you borrow money, or if you receive a loan from either or both of your parents, pay it back within the time frame you agreed upon. One of the worst things you can do is to establish a record of not being reliable. A good rule of thumb is to earn money rather than borrow it. You might be able to do a job or task that your parents may be willing to pay you for. It is better, however, if you seek outside ways of earning money for yourself to cover your own needs and expenses, if at an appropriate age.

Pay your debts by the agreed upon time. Make sure, by all means, you pay your outstanding debts. Your parents may not complain about an outstanding debt, but they will not forget that you owe them. If you think you won't be able to meet the agreed terms, let them know in advance. Parents do not like any unexpected surprises. Establish credibility and maintain a good reputation. By doing this, your parents will not hesitate helping you the next time around.

If you cause unexpected expenses, it could negatively affect your relationship. When your family is on a tight budget, they don't need to get additional bills they are unaware of. You might have heard of instances where unexpected expenses caused by children started serious arguments with their parents.

My wife and I had to make a serious decision concerning our home telephone use. Over and over, our children would make long distance phone calls and receive collect calls from their friends without thinking about the fact that someone had to pay for these expenses. We told them that unauthorized long distance and collect calls were not acceptable, because we could not afford to pay for these kinds of expenses. Confronting them about our concerns did not correct their disregard for us. Subsequently, we had to notify the

110

telephone company to alter our long distance service , so that we had to use a secret password to access long distance service. This was not the kind of action we wanted to take. But, we had to make a decision to correct a problem created by our children. We had to rearrange our situation because of their inconsiderate behavior.

PROMOTE THE FAMILY

Become your own advertising agent. Make your parents aware of the good grades you make in school, the new job promotion, the raise you just received, or even your room you've cleaned up. When you are in public or private settings, be on your best behavior. Conduct yourself in a respectful and polite way. Be patient and courteous. Open the door for your parents. Help them with their seats. Help them with their coats. Carry their bags, if they have any. Look for as many ways as you can to show how considerate and helpful you can be. Being helpful and polite gives your parents and others a reason to recognize you for your outstanding behavior.

VISIT THEM OR CALL

Visit or call your parents at least once a day, just to speak to them or ask if there's anything you can do for them. This will offset the times in which you have called them asking for help. Mom and dad won't mind you calling for assistance if you have been calling all along to see how they are doing.

LET THEM CATCH YOU DOING THINGS RIGHT!

Mom and dad may not make favorable decisions, if they are unaware of your positive actions. Remember, your good deeds always outweigh your bad ones. Help your parents become aware of your ability to solve your own problems, and even other family problems. How can you help your parents become aware of this? Simply by bringing your brothers and sisters closer together as a family. Teaching and guiding your brothers and sisters by setting good examples is another way. ***Teach them the techniques for managing their parents!*** Encourage them to be obedient and grateful. These are very effective ways for receiving credit for what you do.

111

DO THE LITTLE THINGS

Be willing to go the extra yard, not necessarily a mile. You can make progress one step at a time if you remember the simple things in life. Do the extra little things which will get you favorable responses from your parents.

Pick up your clothes or pieces of paper that may be on the floor. Lock the doors which might have been left opened by other family members. Clean off the table after a good meal prepared by mom and dad. Be willing to assist your brothers and sisters when they are helping your parents. Always be involved when the opportunity comes to work with your family.

HONOR THY FATHER AND THY MOTHER

Never do anything that will cause embarrassment or bring shame to your family. Make sure your school conduct and grades are good. Keeping your grades acceptable and your conduct above reproach is absolutely essential. Your teachers should never get a chance to notify your parents about anything negative concerning you. Remember, mom and dad work on their jobs to support you. They do not need to spend valuable time on something negative you have done. If you want your parents to see how well you are doing in school, ask your teachers for letters of your progress. Ask your teachers to make phone calls to your parents letting them know about your school performance. This works miracles! Sometimes, your teachers may procrastinate with your request. So be polite but persistent.

Perform good deeds with integrity, honesty, and sincerity. Integrity is the foundation of trust which is essential for you as a manager. Trust is very powerful in a relationship. It motivates people to do their best, believing that they will be treated fairly. As a manager you must *walk the talk.* You can state integrity in two words, *"build trust."*

Making Mistakes - You make mistakes. And when you do, view them as learning experiences to be turned into successes. Always make safe and sound decisions for you and your parents. Your decision making, whether good or bad, is a reflection of you. So, give your parents a good impression of you whenever the opportunity presents itself.

Just make sure you live up to the expectations you have set for yourself. This technique will work very well in getting your parents to trust you with responsibilities. Be reliable and trustworthy. Make your parents aware of the things they should know in advance, whenever possible. Never let your parents down, and be more than willing to assist them always.

ACCEPT THEM UNCONDITIONALLY

Accept your parents as they are. Accept their fears, anxieties, and idiosyncrasies (habits, modes of expression, or mannerisms) unconditionally. That means without prejudice or judgment. They may or may not be the wealthiest, most attractive, well-educated, or popular people around. But, with God's help, they have birthed you into this world and this qualifies them for unconditional acceptance and love.

TRUST

With authority comes responsibility, and with responsibility comes trust. Establish trust with your parents. Notice how others gain the trust of your parents. What is it about the way you behave in the relationship that may cause distrust? Establishing trust is an ongoing process. You may experience a successful relationship with mom and dad. But, sometimes things may go wrong which will cause your parents to doubt their decisions about trusting you. Remain confident! Be patient , get "back on track" and remember setbacks are just part of the process. There may be difficult circumstances that you may have to overcome. But, remember the Qur'an says, "Surely after difficulty comes ease. *Surely after difficulty comes ease. But when thy immediate task has been removed, still strive hard.*" Working to overcome difficulties will always bring you a sense of ease and relief. When you have conquered or overcome those obstacles, be prepared to face the new challenges ahead. This process of overcoming difficulties will allow you to grow and become stronger as an individual. Look forward to new challenges. The rewards are growth and knowledge. Remember, you do not have to have a degree in psychology, sociology, or counseling in order to manage your parents.

You can learn and master these proven, practical techniques as well as anyone else. You may be challenged in your first attempt to managing your parents in certain areas, but reassess your efforts so you can make the proper decisions next time.

MAKE THE RELATIONSHIP FUNFUL!

Make the relationship "funful". This is a word I made-up which means full of fun. Celebrating birthdays, anniversaries, and other special achievements are a few good ways to add fun to the family. Looking at family photos or videos, story-telling, listening to music, playing games, and dancing are some additional ways of having fun with family. No matter what you do in order to have fun, make your parents and other family members feel like winners! Parents love to relate to their children. This gives them a feeling of success and enjoyment. If you doubt these methods work, look at the millions of dollars spent on sports and other fun-filled activities everyday. These events and activities allow people to have fun and experience a feeling of "winning". They have a great influence on motivation and are therapeutic. Making your family's environment "funful" will establish, as well as maintain, positive growth and participation.

YOUR PARENTS ARE ALWAYS RIGHT

View your parents as if they were your customers. Remember, the attitude of a successful business is, "the customer is always right." This kind of attitude maintains a positive relationship with the customer by meeting their needs. This same attitude will work with mom and dad. Remember Parent:

- *Rule #1: "Your parents are always right!"*
- *Rule #2: "If you think your parents are wrong, see rule number one."*

This may come as a complete surprise to them if this is the first time you have ever used this technique. Your parents may become a little suspicious and inquisitive about your actions. But believe me, this techniques works!

PART 12

MAINTAINING A GOOD
RELATIONSHIP WITH PARENTS

KNOW WHAT TO DO AND HOW TO DO IT

It is important to know what to do, but just as important to know how to do it. If you are told to shoot a ball in a basket while playing the game of basketball, you must first know how to do it. Knowing how to do what you are supposed to do, is extremely important. How do you maintain a good relationship with mom and dad? Here are some suggestions.

TIE YOUR CAMEL

There is a saying that reads, *"tie your camel."* It simply means if you do not tie your camel, your camel will walk away or someone may take him away. If you do not maintain a good relationship with your parents it will fade away. It will not continue to grow and improve. Some children know how to establish lasting relationships. They intuitively understand the importance other people play in their lives. Other than the Creator, your relationships are the most important facet of your life. Since most people who are considered successful are those who build good relationships with others, you need to know how they accomplish this.

NOURISH THE RELATIONSHIP

Once you have established a good relationship with your parents, *tie it up!* Secure the relationship, by protecting it with truth and honesty. Nourish the relationship by being proactive with positive deeds. Find ways to improve the relationship. Secure the relationship so it will not unravel. Maintaining the relationship establishes a basis for future improvement and growth. The more you nourish and maintain the relationship with your parents, the better it becomes. All human beings need attention like flowers need sunshine and rain. Give your parents as much attention as possible.

RELAXING TOO SOON IS DANGEROUS

You cannot "relax too soon" or become "laid back" after experiencing success with managing your parents. Remember change is going to come and managing change is an ongoing process. Being a visionary will help you to identify the opportunities that come with change. Ask yourself questions, such as, who, what, when, why, how, and where change may be coming. Being attentive to change will help you keep your skills sharpened so that maintenance of the relationship is easy.

Make people feel good about being around you. Treat others the way you want to be treated all the time. Listen closely to others' concerns. Show how you value and care for them. All successful, high-achieving men and women know how to establish and maintain long-lasting relationships with other people. Studies show that people are more apt to stay in relationships when there is a genuine like for one another. They make people feel comfortable and natural when others are around them. Being content and making your parents feel content is one of the ways you can start helping them feel comfortable around you.

ESTABLISH RAPPORT

The most important thing about establishing rapport and developing and maintaining your relationship is knowing exactly what your goal is. You must identify, exactly, what you want in the relationship. You can avoid misunderstandings and confusion by setting goals for the relationship.

Research shows about 85 percent of your achievements in life come from interacting with other people. Your self-esteem, your personality and your self-image are expressions of the quality of the relationship you have with others. If you can increase your ability to get along with your parents, you will enjoy the wonderful results of your efforts.

BECOME INTERESTED IN THEM

The best way to get your parents to become interested in you is to become interested in them. The best way to get your parents to believe in you is to believe in them. The best way to get your parents to trust in you is to trust them. The best way to get your parents to like you or to love you is to love them. The best way to get your parents to be your friend is to be their friend. If you want your parents to respect you, respect them.

The biblical commands to *"Do unto to others as you will have others to do unto you... cast your bread upon the water and you will see it return to you... as ye sow, so shall ye reap,"* are clear indications that you must make an investment in your parents. Take the initiative to better the relationship and look for "good" in every opportunity and for every situation. When you can get along with your parents, your self-esteem will increase, and so will your parents'.

You will find that your self-esteem is tied to your ability to enjoy loving relationships with others, especially your parents. The feeling of having a good relationship will cause you and your parents to experience happiness.

MOM AND DAD COME FIRST

Always help your parents before you help someone else's parents. Your parents may feel insecure, if your relationship with other people's parents appear to be better than your relationship with them. Remember, your mother and father are human beings with sensitivities and emotions. They may not express a feeling of jealousy openly, but it may exist when it appears that you are paying more attention to others.

SHOW GRATITUDE

Be sincere and genuine when you give mom and dad recognition. To avoid coming across as insincere, recognize your parents' decision making and leadership only every now and then. Approve and recognize their good deeds immediately. You may forget to high-light what they have done if you wait too late or become distracted.

You will find, as a result, that your parents will do more and more to receive recognition for their deeds and decisions, just as you are doing. Let your parents know they are your role models. Every parent wants to hear that from their children.

LISTEN

As you learned in the chapter on Communication, listening builds trust within the relationship. It is a technique that requires a conscious effort on your part. Concentrate, on what is being said when your parents are talking to you. Again, this raises their self-esteem and, in turn, your self-esteem also rises. Lean forward when listening. Acknowledge your attentiveness by shaking your head in a positive way. Acknowledge your listening with an occasional "okay", "yes sir" or "yes ma'am." If you have to respond to their comments or questions, as a rule, pause before replying. This gives your parents the impression you are paying attention and giving them careful consideration.

Remember that you can enhance your listening skills by using reflective listening. If your parents ask you a question or make a comment that requires a response, repeat the question or comment before you answer it. This will allow them to hear themselves. It will give them an opportunity check their communication. This technique will convey to them you are really paying attention. Ask open ended questions like, "What do you mean? How can I...? Who is....? When will ...? Why?" during the conversation.   These kind of questions allows parents to emphasize main points. It also allows them to "open up."

NEVER CRITICIZE

Never criticize your parents for any reason. There is nothing you can get out of negative criticism. I say negative criticism because I believe there is no such thing as constructive criticism. You may think criticizing your parents will get you positive results, but it will not. It will only give you negative results and a negative attitude from mom and dad.

When someone criticizes you, does it make you feel good? No. It only makes you feel bad or sad, and sometimes angry that you did not live up to others' expectations. Criticizing them lowers their self-esteem and as always, in the law of sowing and reaping, you lower your own. Eliminate criticism from your frame of mind.

What do you do when your parents criticize you or make observations of your deficient behavior? While criticism and pointing out your deficiencies are not positive messages, learn from these remarks and take corrective action. There are many things you can do to manage this opportunity. First, take any criticism as an area which needs improving. Remember, do not take any of their negative observations personally, whether they are right or wrong. Take these observations as being their honest opinions. This is one way to receive feedback of how you are doing in their eyesight. This simply gives you a chance to improve the relationship in addition to your expectations.

THE SEVEN REQUIREMENTS FOR SUCCESS

Finally, I want to give to you what I consider to be the *seven requirements for success.* When we examine how a human being lives and what makes him or her successful, these seven things always appear.

Number one

The number one requirement for success is God Almighty. *"From whence cometh my help, my help cometh from the Lord, who created the heavens and the earth." "Man shall not live by bread alone, but by every word that proceedeth out of the mouth of God."* We must remember that all of our help comes from a higher source, God. We must put God first in everything we do. If we ask for God's assistance first, then success can be expected and achieved. God, the Almighty is the *absolute key, main ingredient, the essential* for all the success we experience or will be experiencing. This is the reason why I say, "God is the number one requirement for success."

Number Two

The second requirement for success is having clear and established goals. When we study the lives of the most successful people, we find out they had specific goals which drove them toward their desires.

Number Three

The third requirement for success is good health. If you want to find out how important good health is, ask someone who is sick or injured. Good health provides us with the energy we will need in order to achieve our goals.

Number Four

The fourth requirement for success is loving and friendly relationships. Your loved ones, friends and other family members are the people who can support you when times become difficult and celebrate your joy. Loved ones and friends can be your "bridge over troubled waters" when situations get rough. We all need loved ones and friends to empathize, console and encourage us. We all require love from others like "flowers need rain."

Number Five

The fifth requirement for success is self-actualization. That is simply finding yourself in life; finding the things you love to do seven days a week without pay. Finding your place in life means doing the things you want to do and those things which make you happy, satisfied, and fulfilled as a human being.

Number Six

The sixth requirement for success is financial freedom. You cannot become "rich" or "independent" working for someone else. Your condition could become better if you're at the highest level of your organization or company, making a "top" salary. However, if you want to become financially independent so you won't have to worry about money, it means becoming an entrepreneur.

Number Seven

Finally, the seventh requirement for success is *peace of mind.* Peace of mind means freedom from fear, freedom from failure, freedom from guilt, and freedom from anger. If you have God as a number one priority in your life; if you have clear and specific goals; if you have loving and friendly relationships with others; if you have reaching self-actualization; if you have financial freedom, you have "peace of mind."

After all isn't this what God wants us to achieve in our lives as human beings. *Peace, Salaam, Shalom and yes, you are a happy person when you are at this level in your life.*

SUMMARY

Ask the Creator to help you. Make a decision to change. Follow the steps in goal setting. Learn the roles of a manager. Learn to be an effective communicator. Implement the strategies for managing your parents. Motivate your parents by creating the environment in which they can motivate themselves. Become a favorite child. Engage in an ongoing process of personal development. Understand what kind of parents you have. Remember to be polite and courteous. Be kind to your parents, relatives, friends, teachers, classmates, supervisors, co-workers, those who live in poverty, the young, the old, the helpless, and the people you see from day to day. And remember, God has made it a duty for you to be obedient and good to your parents.

Never say cruel and disobedient things to them, nor be harsh to them, But speak to them kindly. Serve them with tenderness and humility.

Make a list of 100 things that will make your parents happy. Do what you're supposed to do, when you should do it, no matter what the circumstances are. If it's to be, it's up to you.

EPILOGUE

Knowledge is power, if you remember to use it.

I asked God Almighty to guide my thoughts in conveying to you the knowledge of how to manage your parents. I have given this project my best effort so that you can improve the relationship you have with your parents. You have been exposed to some of the greatest knowledge available to better your conditions. Research shows if you read something at least six times a year, you will become an authority on that particular subject. I encourage you to read this book over and over again so you can perfect your skills. Work everyday to manage your parents and it will become almost effortless. Satisfied parents are the best friends you can ever have. Now that you know how to mange your parents, go on and do it!

General
Bibliography

Ali, Abdullah Yusuf. *Holy Qur'an.* Lahore, Pakistan: Sh. Muhammad
Ashraf, 1981.

Ali, Mulana M. *Holy Qur'an.* Lahore, Pakistan: The Ahmadiyyah
Anjuman Isha'at Islam, 1963.

Black, James M. *How to Grow in Management.* Englewood
Cliffs, NJ: Prentice Hall, Inc., 1957.

Brown, Les. *You Deserve.* Chicago: Televideo, 1990. Videocassette.

Child Magazine. 1993-1995.

Dawson, Roger. *The Secret of Power Negotiating.* Chicago:
Nightingale Conant Corp., 1987. Audiocassette.

Ewing, David W. *The Managerial Mind.* Toronto: The Macmillian
Co., 1964

Fast, Julius. *Body Language.* New York: Pocket Books, 1977.

Hegarty, Christopher. *How To Manage Your Boss.* New York: Simon
& Schuster Audio Publishing, 1986. Audiocassette.

Hiring & Firing. Kansas City, MO: Padgett/Thompson Audio
Publishing, 1987. Audiocassette.

Holy Bible. King James version. N.p.: The National Publishing Co.,
1972.

Key, Wilson B. *Subliminal Seduction.* New York: The New
American Library, 1974.

Lakein, Alan. *How to Take Control of Your Time.* New York: David
McKay Co., 1973.

LeBoueuf, Michael. *How To Win Customers and Keep Them For
Life.* New York: G.P. Putnam's Sons, 1987.

Longenecker, Justin G. *The Principles of Management and
Organizational Behavior.* Columbus, OH: Charles E. Merrill
Publishing Co., 1969.

Muhammad, Elijah. *How To Eat To Live.* Chicago: Muhammad
Mosque of Islam #2, 1967.

Muhammad, Warith Deen. *An African American Genesis*. Chicago: Progression Publishing Co., 1986.

——————. *As The Light Shineth From the East*. Chicago: WDM Publishing Co., 1980.

Naisbitt, John. *Megatrends*. New York: Warner Books, 1984.

The Psychology of Success. Volumes 1, 2, and 3. Chicago: Nightingale Conant Corp., 1986. Videocassette.

Pulos, Lee. *The Power of Visualization*. Chicago: Nightingale Conant Corp., 1993. Audiocassette.

Smalley, Gary. *Hidden Keys To Successful Parenting*. Paoli, PA: Relationships Today, Inc., 1991. Videocassette.

Smith, Malcolm E. *With Love From Dad*. Smithown, NY: Suffolk House, n.d.

Supervising for Results. Kansas City, MO: Sourcecom, 1988. Videocassette.

Tracy, Brian. *The Psychology of Achievement*. Chicago: Nightingale Conant Corp., 1986. Audiocassette.

Van Fleet, James K. *Conversation Power*. Chicago: Nightingale Conant Corp., 1990. Audiocassette.

Waitley, Dennis. *The Psychology of Winning*. Chicago: Nightingale Conant Corp., 1987. Audio and video cassettes.

What The Pros Say About Success. Kansas City, MO: Sourcecom Audio Cassettes Series, 1989. Audiocassette.

Ziggler, Zig. *Goal & Goal Achieving*. Chicago: Nightingale Conant Corp., 1986. Videocassette.

SURVEY

Dear reader:

We would appreciate hearing from you about KYD Publishers nonfiction book. It will allow us to continue to give you the best quality reading possible. Please take your time and complete or check the appropriate area. Thanks.

1. What most influenced you to purchase the How To Manage Your Parents book ?

__Author
__Subject Matter
__Backcover copy
__Cover/Title
__Recommendations

__ _____

2. Where did you purchase this book?

__Bookstore
__Department Store
__Grocery Store
__Book signing
__Mail order

__ _____

3. Your overall rating of this book?

__Excellent
__Very good
__Good
__Fair
__Poor

Comments or Why the rating?

_____

_____

4. How likely would you be to purchase other books by this author?

__Very likely
__Somewhat likely
__Not very likely
__Not at all

5. Please check the box next to your age group.

__Under 13
__13 - 20
__21 - 25
__26 - 30
__31 - 35
__36 - 40
__41 - 45
__46 - 50
__55 - 60
__60 - Over

6. Month you purchased this book.?

_____

Please Mail to:
KYD Publishers
401 Hillside Drive, S.W.
Atlanta, GA 30310
Fax # 404-753-4323 or
Call (404) 752-8877

NOTES